The UN Security Council (2006)
Practice and promise
*by Edward C. Luck (Columbia
University)*

**The World Intellectual Property
Organization (2006)**
Resurgence and the development
agenda
*by Chris May (University of
Lancaster)*

**The North Atlantic Treaty
Organization (2007)**
The enduring alliance
*by Julian Lindley-French (European
Union Centre for Security Studies)*

**The International Monetary Fund
(2007)**
Politics of conditional lending
*by James Raymond Vreeland (Yale
University)*

The Group of 7/8 (2007)
*by Hugo Dobson (University of
Sheffield)*

The World Economic Forum (2007)
A multi-stakeholder approach to
global governance
*by Geoffrey Allen Pigman
(Bennington College)*

**The International Committee of the
Red Cross**
A unique humanitarian actor
*by David Forsythe (University
of Nebraska) and
Barbara Ann Rieffer-Flanagan
(Central Washington University)*

**UN Conference on Trade and
Development**
*by Ian Taylor (University of St.
Andrews)*

A Crisis of Global Institutions?
Multilateralism and international
security
*by Edward Newman (United Nations
University)*

The World Bank
From reconstruction to development
to equity
*by Katherine Marshall (Georgetown
University)*

The African Union
Past and future governance challenges
*by Samuel M. Makinda (Murdoch
University) and Wafula Okumu
(McMaster University)*

**Organisation for Economic
Co-operation and Development**
*by Richard Woodward (University of
Hull)*

**Non-Governmental Organizations in
Global Politics**
*by Peter Willetts (City University,
London)*

Multilateralism in the South
An analysis
*by Jacqueline Anne Braveboy-Wagner
(City College of New York)*

The European Union
*by Clive Archer (Manchester
Metropolitan University)*

**The International Labour
Organization**
*by Steve Hughes (University of
Newcastle)*

**The Commonwealth(s) and Global
Governance**
*by Timothy Shaw (Royal Roads
University)*

The Organization for Security and Co-operation in Europe
by David J. Galbreath (University of Aberdeen)

UNHCR
The politics and practice of refugee protection into the twenty-first century
by Gil Loescher (University of Oxford), James Milner (University of Oxford), and Alexander Betts (University of Oxford)

The World Health Organization
by Kelley Lee (London School of Hygiene and Tropical Medicine)

The World Trade Organization
by Bernard Hoekman (World Bank) and Petros Mavroidis (Columbia University)

The International Organization for Standardization and the Global Economy
Setting standards
by Craig Murphy (Wellesley College) and JoAnne Yates (Massachusetts Institute of Technology)

The International Olympic Committee
by Jean-Loup Chappelet (IDHEAP Swiss Graduate School of Public Administration) and Brenda Kübler-Mabbott

For further information regarding the series, please contact:

Craig Fowlie, Publisher, Politics & International Studies
Taylor & Francis
2 Park Square, Milton Park, Abingdon
Oxfordshire OX14 4RN, UK

+44 (0)207 842 2057 Tel
+44 (0)207 842 2302 Fax

craig.fowlie@tandf.co.uk
www.routledge.com

The International Monetary Fund
Politics of conditional lending

James Raymond Vreeland

Routledge
Taylor & Francis Group

LONDON AND NEW YORK

First published 2007
by Routledge
2 Park Square, Milton Park, Abingdon, Oxon OX14 4RN

Simultaneously published in the USA and Canada
by Routledge
270 Madison Avenue, New York, NY 10016

Routledge is an imprint of the Taylor & Francis Group, an informa business

© 2007 James Raymond Vreeland

Typeset in Times New Roman by
Taylor & Francis Books
Printed and bound in Great Britain by
MPG Books Ltd, Bodmin

British Library Cataloguing in Publication Data
A catalogue record for this book is available from the British Library

Library of Congress Cataloging in Publication Data
Vreeland, James Raymond, 1971–
    The International Monetary Fund: politics of conditional lending /
James Raymond Vreeland.
        p. cm.
    Includes bibliographical references and index.
    1. International Monetary Fund. 2. International finance –
    Government policy. 3. International finance. I. Title.
HG3881.5.I58V743 2006
332.1′52 – dc22   2006021855

ISBN10: 0–415–37462–6   ISBN13: 978–0–415–37462–0 (hbk)
ISBN10: 0–415–37463–4   ISBN13: 978–0–415–37463–7 (pbk)
ISBN10: 0–203–96278–8   ISBN13: 978–0–203–96278–7 (ebk)

For Jodi Kaplan, Matthew Milowsky, Douglas Scherr, and especially Daniel and Jeffrey Yao.

Thank you.

Contents

Illustrations

Boxes

Foreword

The current volume is the tenth in a new and dynamic series on "global institutions." The series strives (and, based on the initial volumes we believe, succeeds) to provide readers with definitive guides to the most visible aspects of what we know as "global governance." Remarkable as it may seem, there exist relatively few books that offer in-depth treatments of prominent global bodies and processes, much less an entire series of concise and complementary volumes. Those that do exist are either out of date, inaccessible to the non-specialist reader, or seek to develop a specialized understanding of particular aspects of an institution or process rather than offer an overall account of its functioning. Similarly, existing books have often been written in highly technical language or have been crafted "in-house" and are notoriously self-serving and narrow.

The advent of electronic media has helped by making information, documents, and resolutions of international organizations more widely available, but it has also complicated matters. The growing reliance on the Internet and other electronic methods of finding information about key international organizations and processes has served, ironically, to limit the educational materials to which most readers have ready access – namely, books. Public relations documents, raw data, and loosely refereed web sites do not make for intelligent analysis. Official publications compete with a vast amount of electronically available information, much of which is suspect because of its ideological or self-promoting slant. Paradoxically, the growing range of purportedly independent web sites offering analyses of the activities of particular organizations have emerged, but one inadvertent consequence has been to frustrate access to basic, authoritative, critical, and well-researched texts. The market for such has actually been reduced by the ready availability of varying quality electronic materials.

For those of us who teach, research, and practice in the area, this access to information has been at best frustrating. We were delighted, then, when Routledge saw the value of a series that bucks this trend and provides key reference points to the most significant global institutions. They are betting that serious students and professionals will want serious analyses. We have assembled a first-rate line-up of authors to address that market. Our intention, then, is to provide one-stop shopping for all readers – students (both undergraduate and postgraduate), interested negotiators, diplomats, practitioners from nongovernmental and intergovernmental organizations, and interested parties alike – seeking information about most prominent institutional aspects of global governance.

The International Monetary Fund

Few global institutions can claim to be quite as controversial as the IMF (though the World Bank and the World Trade Organization – both subjects of books forthcoming in this series – come close). Although widely berated by civil society organizations, development economists and governments alike for imposing austerity policies on countries already close to the economic bone, getting it wrong during the Asian financial crisis and an unwavering belief in the capacity of markets to correct their own failures – among other things – little is known about what precisely the organization does, the manner in which it functions, and the ways its role has changed over time. Most accounts of the IMF tend to focus on the wartime discussions that sought to put in place a series of economic institutions designed to reconstruct a war ravaged and depression weary global economy out of which the IMF was created; the way in which the work of the IMF was circumscribed during its early years by the Marshall Plan; and the way in which the IMF and its sibling the World Bank became lenders to the developing world. Or else, they dwell on the economic theory under-pinning the work of the IMF without explaining the operation of the organization, its day to day functioning, or the impact and criticisms of its policies. Yet beyond these well trodden paths there is much that is important to understanding the IMF.

We asked James Vreeland – an Associate Professor in the Department of Political Science at Yale University – to write a book on the IMF for us precisely because we wanted an account that not only provided readers with a definitive guide to the organization but which would also deal with the more demanding aspects of the institution in a clear,

Acknowledgments

For helpful comments, the author is grateful to Mark Choi, Bessma Momani, Terry Musiyambiri, Sebastian Saiegh, Leanna Sudhof, Barry Williams, and especially Axel Dreher, who read the entire manuscript. The author is thankful as well to his colleagues in the Department of Political Science at Yale University – the depth of their support is truly amazing. The author also wishes to thank the editors of the series, Thomas G. Weiss and Rorden Wilkinson, who provided not only many useful suggestions and efficient help with the manuscript, but also personal support. For administrative and financial support, the author acknowledges the MacMillan Center for International and Area Studies at Yale; the UCLA International Institute Global Fellows Program; the Swiss Federal Institute of Technology (ETH), Zurich; and the University of Puerto Rico, Río Piedras. Finally, special thanks are due to the many students who have taken my IMF and other International Relations courses over the years. Their contributions to class have helped shape this book.

Abbreviations

BOP	Balance of Payments
EFF	Extended Fund Facility
ESAF	Extended Structural Adjustment Facility
GDP	Gross Domestic Product
GNI	Gross National Income
IEO	Independent Evaluations Office
IMF	International Monetary Fund
LOI	Letter of Intent
MONA	Monitoring Fund Arrangements
PPP	Purchasing Power Parity
PRGF	Poverty Reduction and Growth Facility
PRSP	Poverty Reduction Strategy Paper
SAF	Structural Adjustment Facility
SBA	Stand-by Arrangement
SDR	Special Drawing Rights
UN	United Nations
US	United States

Introduction

At the writing of this book, 49 developing countries around the world – whose populations account for more than one billion people – are participating in economic programs supported by the International Monetary Fund (IMF or Fund).[1] These "IMF programs" grant the governments of these countries access to IMF loans, but access to the loans can be cut off if the governments fail to comply with specific policy conditions. IMF policy conditions impact the lives of individuals living in these countries in intimate ways: the policy conditions address government expenditures, so IMF programs help determine whether roads, schools, or debt repayment take priority. The policy conditions also address interest rates, so they may affect one's ability to borrow to purchase a home or invest in a business. IMF policy conditions often address the value of the national currency, so IMF programs may impact the very purchasing power of the money in people's pockets.

Not surprisingly, the IMF is well known throughout the developing world – to the elites and the masses alike. The organization often appears to exercise as much or even more authority than their own governments. Yet, the IMF is less familiar to average citizens in the developed world. And, to many throughout the world, the actual functioning of the organization is unknown or misunderstood. Unfounded opinion about the IMF abounds among people who often lump it together with other international institutions like the World Bank and the World Trade Organization, even though the administration and purposes of the IMF are quite distinct from these other international institutions.

Founded in the wake of the Great Depression, the IMF can be thought of as an international credit union with access to a pool of resources provided by the subscriptions of its members, which include nearly every country in the world. The size of a country's contribution depends on the country's economic dominance, hence, the bulk of the resources of the IMF come from the developed world. The Fund can lend from this pool of resources to countries facing economic problems. These days, the only countries that borrow from the IMF come from the developing world.

IMF loans can be thought of as a form of insurance for governments against the possibility of an economic crisis. Such insurance, however, introduces something economists call "moral hazard": the prospect of receiving assistance in the face of an economic crisis in the form of an IMF loan may itself lower a government's incentive to avoid the bad economic policies that cause economic crises in the first place.

To counter moral hazard, the IMF imposes *conditionality*: governments are required to follow what the IMF deems as "good" policies in return for the continued disbursements of the IMF loan. Thus, one can think of an IMF program as having two components: the *loan* and the *conditions* attached to the loan. The goal of this arrangement is to first stabilize a country facing a balance of payments crisis and then to promote growth and the reduction of poverty.

Yet, conditionality is controversial. If the policies imposed by the IMF are so good for countries, why must governments be enticed through conditional lending? At the heart of this question is national sovereignty, and beyond purely economic guidelines, the imposition of IMF programs is heavily influenced by international and domestic politics.

International politics play a role because powerful members sometimes use their influence at the IMF to pursue political goals. Votes at the IMF, like contributions, are pegged to a country's economic size, so economically powerful countries have more say at the IMF than other countries, and can pressure the Fund to do their bidding. Governments who are considered important allies of the IMF's most influential members – like the United States – sometimes receive preferential treatment from the IMF. The IMF may bail them out of economic crises with large loans even if they fail to comply with IMF conditions of changing economic policy.

Yet, at the domestic level of politics in developing countries, there are other cases where governments actually want IMF conditions to be imposed. These governments seek the assistance of the international institution to get around domestic political constraints and force changes in economic policy. Governments can use IMF conditionality to gain leverage over domestic opposition to policy change. Sometimes, such policy changes result in superior outcomes for society, but often IMF leverage is used to protect elites and make others bear the cost of an economic crisis.

Unfortunately, there is scant evidence of the success of IMF conditionality. Studies have even found that IMF programs hurt economic growth. A further effect of IMF programs is the increase of income inequality. This is not just because the IMF is involved with countries that already have economic problems – even accounting for this fact, these disappointing results hold.

There is little consensus over why IMF programs have the perverse effects that they do. Some argue that the influence of international political pressures has led to low levels of compliance with IMF conditionality. As a result, IMF lending simply subsidizes the continuation of bad economic policies. Others argue that the economic policies imposed by the IMF are the wrong ones. Instead of imposing austerity, the IMF should promote economic stimulus packages so that developing countries can grow their way out of economic problems. Still others argue that failure is due to domestic politics. Policy may change under IMF programs, but governments implement only selected reforms or impose partial reform with the goal of insulating domestic political elites and placing the burden of the economic crisis on labor and the poor. Strangely, with all of these various points of view, there is a broad based consensus that the IMF should scale back its operations. Many feel that the IMF should get out of the development business.

Recently, however, the IMF has made a bold new commitment to promote economic development through continued conditional lending. Thus, IMF programs remain a presence throughout most of the developing world. In some countries, participation in IMF programs is business as usual, a routine way of life. This book thus explores IMF conditional lending – its origins, effects, and future.

The chapters ahead address many questions – not the least of which is whether the IMF has been successful. The book – an introduction to the international and domestic politics of IMF programs – is appropriate for beginning students of international relations and is also intended for the policy making and NGO communities, as well as people familiar with the economics of IMF programs but less familiar with the political science literature on the subject. The first chapter introduces IMF programs and describes the IMF's history, functioning, and organization. Subsequent chapters pose specific questions: Chapter 2 (Who controls the IMF?) examines the international politics of IMF lending and conditionality. Chapter 3 (Why do governments participate in IMF programs?) explores the domestic politics of IMF conditionality. Chapter 4 (What are the effects of IMF programs?) reviews the success, or lack thereof, of IMF programs. This chapter also tackles the difficult question of how to evaluate IMF effectiveness, given that its economic reform programs are prescribed only to the economically sickest of patient-countries. Chapter 5 (Do governments comply with IMF programs?) turns to the frontier of research on the IMF – whether governments actually comply with what the IMF requires in its arrangements. The answer is not obvious because of the opacity of the international institution. Chapter 6 (Reform the IMF?) presents the debate about reforming the IMF. The chapter questions the policies included in IMF programs and the level of enforcement of conditionality, as well as questioning whether the IMF should be involved in the business of economic development at all. Chapter 7 provides an overall review of the book, and takes a step back to consider not just *what* the IMF should do better, but *why* one should expect the IMF to bother to do better. The chapter addresses the incentives of the IMF.

1 What is the IMF?

The origin of the IMF

On July 22, 1944 – in the aftermath of the Great Depression – 44 countries signed the "Bretton Woods Agreements" establishing the International Monetary Fund and its sister organization, the International Bank for Reconstruction and Development (now commonly known as the World Bank).[1] The agreements were so-named after the Mount Washington Hotel at Bretton Woods, New Hampshire – the ski resort that hosted the International Monetary Conference of the United and Associated Nations, where the negotiations over the design of these two international institutions took place. The IMF and the World Bank have since come to be known as the "Bretton Woods" institutions. On December 27, 1945, after 29 countries had ratified the IMF Articles of Agreement, the IMF came into force.

Interestingly, the reason the IMF was formed has little to do with the economic programs in developing countries for which the IMF is famous today. Originally, the IMF was intended to monitor and help maintain pegged but adjustable exchange rates, primarily between the industrialized countries of Western Europe and the United States. The task of promoting economic development – development for war-torn Europe – was assigned to the institution that has come to be known as the World Bank. Also negotiated at the Bretton Woods Conference was an agreement that grew into the General Agreement on Tariffs and Trade and eventually became the World Trade Organization, which was assigned the task of promoting freer trade among countries.

Why was an institution like the IMF deemed necessary? In an earlier era, during the end of the nineteenth century, countries had been on a strict "gold standard" of foreign exchange. The national currencies of different countries were all convertible into gold held on reserve by governments. This gold standard enforced discipline in the

Box 1.1 The original members of the IMF

The Articles of Agreement of the International Monetary Fund entered into force on December 27, 1945. By December 31, 35 countries had signed and otherwise indicated their intention to become members. These original members of the IMF (reported in the *Summary Proceedings of the First Annual Meeting of the Board of Governors*, September 27 to October 3, 1946) were:

Belgium	Iceland
Bolivia	India
Brazil	Iran
Canada	Iraq
Chile	Luxembourg
China	Mexico
Colombia	Netherlands
Costa Rica	Norway
Cuba	Paraguay
Czechoslovakia	Peru
Dominican Republic	Philippine Commonwealth
Ecuador	Poland
Egypt	Union of South Africa
Ethiopia	United Kingdom
France	United States of America
Greece	Uruguay
Guatemala	Yugoslavia
Honduras	

balance of payments between countries. If countries faced a balance of payments deficit – because, for example, the value of its imports exceeded the value of its exports – the requirement to back up domestic currency by gold would force the supply of money down. As a result, demand for imported goods would go down (because their prices would be too high), and the balance would right itself.

This gold standard imposed economic austerity on deficit countries, which was particularly costly to certain groups within these countries. As explained by economist Barry Eichengreen of the University of California, Berkeley, to maintain a fixed exchange rate in the face of a balance of payments deficit, domestic consumption must be cut – this often meant economic growth slowed, and unemployment rose.[2]

As laborers – who were hard hit by such changes – organized into unions and the right to vote was extended towards universal suffrage, resistance mounted against the discipline of the gold standard. Governments sought to avoid the austerity that maintaining the gold standard entailed when facing a balance of payments deficit. This led to all sorts of economic problems during the first half of the twentieth century. For example, some governments faced speculative runs of the national currency, where people exchanged the national currency for gold or for foreign exchange, fearing that the government would not maintain convertibility to gold. The fear that the national currency would lose value could become a self-fulfilling prophecy if enough people fled from the national currency. In the run up to the Great Depression, governments eventually engaged in "beggar-thy-neighbor" currency devaluations and erected barriers to trade to protect themselves from balance of payments problems, at the expense of world prosperity. In an era of democracy, where governments had other domestic priorities that took precedence over maintaining foreign exchange rates, the strict gold standard needed help.

Part of the proposed solution was an international credit union from which countries facing a temporary balance of payments deficit could borrow foreign exchange. Such a loan would allow countries to maintain a fixed exchange rate and soften the blow of austerity as the economy adjusted. Each country's currency would still be backed by gold, but if national reserves of gold or foreign exchange dropped too low, there would be an international lending facility that could provide assistance.

Several specific plans were developed in the early 1940s. The British plan, entitled *Proposals for an International Currency (or Clearing) Union*, was developed by John Maynard Keynes, who was considered to be the greatest economist of his time. Keynes originally proposed the importance of international lending as early as 1919 when he talked of a post-war "international loan."[3] Following the Great Depression, Keynes proposed a "Clearing Union" with access to a pool of resources that could be lent to countries facing balance of payments deficits. Deficit countries would be required to adjust downward their consumption of imports so that deficits would not persist or widen, but loans from the Clearing Union would allow them to do so gradually to avoid domestic hardship. For such a plan to be effective, Keynes envisaged a Clearing Union with access to tremendous resources, particularly from countries with balance of payments surpluses.

In the years leading up to the Bretton Woods conference, the country with the largest surpluses was the United States, and the US was wary of Keynes' plan, viewing it as potentially opening creditor countries up to unlimited liability.[4] The US plan,[5] developed by Treasury economist Harry Dexter White, called for all countries to make contributions to a much smaller "Stabilization Fund" from which countries facing balance of payments deficits could purchase foreign exchange. While the Keynes Plan called for contributions totaling $26 billion (with $23 billion from the US), the White Plan called for only $5 billion (with $2 billion from the US).[6]

These plans along with others – for example, a French plan and a Canadian plan – were negotiated throughout the early 1940s, ultimately resulting in the IMF Articles of Agreement at Bretton Woods. The result turned out to resemble the White Plan more than any of the others. The subscriptions to the IMF totaled $8.8 billion, with just $2.75 billion from the US.[7]

The resources of the newly formed IMF turned out to be insufficient to stabilize the economies and exchange rates of Europe following World War II. Rather than expand the size of the IMF, however, the US took it upon itself to assist directly with the Marshall Plan, providing a total of $13 billion in assistance to Europe between 1947 and 1953. The US wanted to have more control than the IMF would have allowed.

Indeed, the US would only provide Marshall Plan assistance to countries that did not seek additional assistance from the IMF.[8] The IMF was essentially dealt out of the rebuilding process of Europe after World War II – dealt out of the very job the institution was created to perform.

So right from the beginning, the IMF did not play the role that it was created to play. Under the Bretton Woods system, the currencies of IMF members were allowed to fluctuate only within narrow bands. If the value of a currency dropped to the low end of the band, the IMF could and did lend to that country to shore up the currency. Such lending may have softened the blow of adjustment as the country brought down imports and brought up exports, but the problem was that it became increasingly difficult for countries – notably the US – to maintain their currencies in the face of fiscal deficits and expansionary monetary policy. All currencies were monitored closely by the Fund, and any devaluation was supposed to be approved by the IMF, but often countries went ahead on their own. It turned out that when countries failed to maintain their fixed exchange rate, more instability ensued than would have had the currency been allowed to float all along – especially if word leaked that the government intended to approach the IMF about a devaluation of the national currency.

Particularly for industrialized countries, it became clear that market driven exchange rates were a more appealing alternative to the Bretton Woods system.

Eventually, the Bretton Woods system of foreign exchange collapsed. As the mobility of capital and foreign exchange increased in the 1950s and 1960s, it became too difficult and disruptive for developed countries to maintain the gold standard of the Bretton Woods system. In 1971, President Richard Nixon announced that the US would suspend its commitment to exchange dollars for gold. The following two years witnessed two devaluations of the dollar, a speculative attack on the pound sterling, and decisions by Switzerland, Germany, France and several other European countries to float their currencies. By 1973, the adjustable pegged exchange rates of the industrialized world were abandoned forever. The original *raison d'être* of the IMF was gone.

Early involvement in the developing world

Many argue that it was at this point – during the 1970s – that the IMF shifted its attention from the industrialized world to the developing world, as the institution searched for a new purpose. People seem to love to hearken back to the early days of the IMF when it dealt with the industrialized world, not the developing world. A popular myth is that before the 1970s, the IMF engaged in truly temporary lending. Yet, the IMF never played as big a role in industrialized countries as originally intended. And while the very first loans the IMF provided did go to industrialized countries, the Fund began lending to developing countries as early as 1954 – a four year program for Peru began that year. As Figure 1.1 shows, by 1958 the percentage of non-industrial countries participating in IMF programs outpaced the percentage of participation among the US, Japan, and Western Europe. Looking at the actual number of programs, non-industrial countries outpaced industrial countries as early as 1956 (Figure 1.2).

If the IMF was created to facilitate international exchange among industrialized countries, what was the Fund doing in developing countries? From the beginning, the IMF was assigned – broadly speaking – two main tasks: (1) to *monitor* members' economies – especially their exchange rates and balance of payments, and (2) to act as an *international lender*. Broadly speaking, this is what the IMF was doing – and still does – in the developing world. The loans to developing countries were consistent with the IMF mandate to provide balance of payments assistance, but instead of intervening in the exchange rates of the

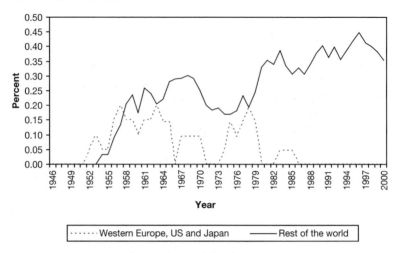

Figure 1.1 Percentage of countries participating in IMF programs.

industrialized nations, it provided assistance – at increasing rates over time – to the developing world from the 1950s onward.

Regarding the task of *monitoring* or "surveillance," the IMF engages in bilateral discussions – called "Article IV consultations" – with nearly every country in the world – developed and developing alike. The Fund examines whether a country's currency is overvalued and whether the exchange rate policies are appropriate. Over time, the

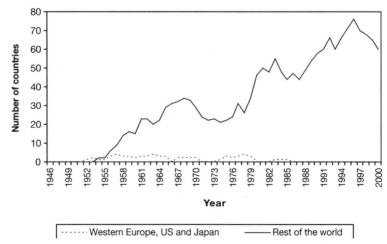

Figure 1.2 Number of countries participating in IMF programs.

IMF has increasingly examined other economic policies. A recent innovation in surveillance is a multilateral dimension, where the economic
connections among countries are considered. The IMF is not as widely
known for its monitoring activities, however, as it is known for its lending
activities.

The IMF's actions as *international lender* are particularly conspic-
uous because when the IMF makes a loan to a government, the loan
usually comes with strings attached. Recall that the Keynes plan called
for gradual adjustment of domestic consumption, lest loans of foreign
exchange finance ever-widening balance of payments deficits. Recall
also the US concerns about unlimited liability for creditor countries. In
the spirit of these concerns, the IMF requires a government to meet
specific *policy conditions* in return for a loan of foreign currency. In
return for the IMF loan, the IMF requires countries to follow austere
economic policies to lower domestic consumption. In this way, the
IMF influences domestic economic policy.

Thus, at the crux of IMF conditioned loans is the national sovereignty of developing countries. Not surprisingly, this is the source of
most of the controversy surrounding the international institution.
"Conditionality" – the practice by which loans are provided to governments in return for compliance with specific policy conditions – is the
focus of many IMF debates, protests, and even riots. It is also the focus
of this book.

So, this chapter returns to "conditionality" below, but – before
going any further – it is time to take a step back and address another
basic question: Who is the IMF?

Box 1.2 Monitoring

Beyond Article IV consultations, the IMF engages in several other
forms of monitoring. For example, many countries have committed
to Article VIII of the IMF Articles of Agreement, which stipulates
that a government will keep the current account free from restric-
tion. The IMF monitors that governments that have signed on to
Article VIII live up to their commitment. This is an interesting
example of international law in that it appears to have a strong
binding impact on the behavior of governments. Beth Simmons, a
political scientist at Harvard University, has found that governments
that commit to Article VIII are significantly less likely to place
restrictions on the current account than countries that do not.[9]

The membership and organization of the IMF

Currently, there are 184 members of the IMF. This is practically the entire world.[10] There are, for example, 191 members of the United Nations; the members of the UN who are not in the IMF are: Andorra, Cuba, Liechtenstein, Monaco, Nauru, North Korea, and Tuvalu. Most of these are small states – so small, they have never even had their own national currency. The exceptions are Cuba and North Korea, which, as discussed below, are not members because of Communism.

Most Communist countries were not members of the IMF during the Cold War. The Soviet Union participated in the 1944 negotiations at Bretton Woods, but did not sign the Articles of Agreement. China also participated at Bretton Woods and became an original IMF member in 1945, but membership was maintained only by the government in Taiwan (Republic of China) after 1949, when mainland China was taken over by the Communist government that continues to rule mainland China today (People's Republic of China). Poland, also an original member of the IMF, withdrew in 1950, citing in its official withdrawal letter to the IMF that the Fund had become "a submissive instrument of the Government of the United States."[11] Another original member, Czechoslovakia, rescinded membership in 1954. Cuba left the IMF in 1964.

There were exceptions, however, and membership from the Communist world grew over the course of the Cold War. Socialist Yugoslavia was an original member and remained a member throughout the Cold War. Romania joined the IMF in 1972. Vietnam joined in 1956 shortly after independence and remained a member even after unification under the Communist north in 1975.[12] Chinese representation at the Fund was transferred from the government in Taiwan to the mainland Chinese government in 1980, after increasingly warming relations between Washington and Beijing.[13] Hungary joined the IMF in 1982, and Poland returned to the Fund in 1986.

Finally, after the fall of Communism, all of Eastern Europe joined the Fund. In the meantime, most Latin American, Asian, and North African states either had been original members or had joined in the early years of the Fund. Most countries of Africa South of the Sahara joined shortly after independence (with some notable and interesting exceptions – see Box 1.3). So, by the 1990s, the IMF had virtually universal membership.

With 184 country-members, how does the IMF make decisions? The Articles of Agreement call for votes of various sorts to be taken – most by simple majority, some by 85 percent super-majorities. Each of the

Box 1.3 African membership exceptions

While most colonized African states joined the IMF soon after independence, notable exceptions are Mozambique, which achieved independence from Portugal in 1975, but did not join the IMF until 1984, and Angola, which also achieved independence from Portugal in 1975, and did not join the IMF until 1989. Both countries suffered through civil war after independence and were Soviet allies. Mozambique joined after the government turned away from Socialism and called for economic reform. Angola joined as Cold War politics ended.

Another African exception is Liberia, which became independent in 1847, but did not join the IMF until 1962. This is particularly interesting because North African independent countries – Libya, Morocco, and Tunisia – joined the IMF in 1958, and Egypt, Ethiopia, and South Africa were original members. Liberia applied for membership as early as 1948 and the application was accepted, but Liberia was unable to deposit the necessary quota by the deadline in 1950 and did not take up membership at that time. Another country, Haiti went through a similar experience, applying in 1949 and ultimately being denied in 1950. Haiti was eventually able to join in 1953, however, much earlier than Liberia.

members of the IMF is allotted votes according to the size of the member's subscription to the IMF. This "capital subscription" or "quota," as it is usually called, is a preset amount of currency that each member contributes to the IMF. Note that the quota is not a donation or a grant, nor is it paid every year. Rather, the quota is held as a deposit at the Fund – like a bank deposit. It even earns interest through the lending activities of the Fund, and it is from this interest that the IMF runs its operations. Thus, the IMF can be thought of as a great big international credit union with all of the countries in the world as members.

Quotas are denoted in Special Drawing Rights, or SDRs, a fictitious currency used by the IMF for accounting purposes. The value of the SDR is determined by a basket of "hard" or especially stable currencies. The SDR was introduced in 1969. Prior to this, the IMF relied on the dollar for accounting purposes, but as the value of the dollar fell in the face of fiscal deficits and expansionary monetary policy in the US, the IMF sought a more stable accounting currency. Before the euro existed, the basket consisted of the American dollar, the German mark, the Japanese yen, the British pound, and the French franc – the euro has come to replace the mark and the franc. By pegging the value of the SDR to this basket of currencies, the SDR is more stable than any of its component parts. One unit of SDR tends to be valued at around $1.25–$1.50.

As mentioned above, voting at the IMF depends on the size of a country's quota. The size of a country's quota is a function of the country's economy. Countries large in economic size – with, for example, a large gross domestic product (GDP) – have larger quotas. But GDP is not the only factor. The volume of current account transactions (basically, transactions involving international trade) and the size of official reserves are also factors. Countries that are important exporters, like Saudi Arabia for example, may have a large quota because their currencies are in high demand. The Saudi economy depends heavily on oil exports, while trade is a much smaller proportion of, say, the Canadian economy. This explains why Saudi Arabia has a larger quota than Canada, even though the Canadian GDP is about four times the Saudi GDP.

Presently, the largest quota – SDR 37 billion – belongs to the United States and accounts for 17.40 percent of the sum total of all quotas. The next largest member is Japan, which contributes 6.24 percent of Fund resources, followed by Germany (6.09 percent), the United Kingdom (5.03 percent), and France (5.03 percent). At the other end of the spectrum is Palau, which has the smallest quota of just SDR 3.1 million. The size of quotas is set by the members of the Fund and is reviewed every five years. Any change must be approved by an 85 percent majority of votes.

Countries that are allowed to contribute more to the IMF have an interest in doing so, since money at the IMF translates directly into votes and influence. Changes in quotas are thus important and must be approved by an 85 percent majority of the membership. Each member is given 250 votes plus one additional vote for every 100,000 SDR contributed as its quota. So while Palau's quota accounts for only 0.001 percent of total contributions, it controls 0.01 percent of the votes. The United States quota is 17.40 percent of total contributions, but it controls 17.08 percent of the votes. Note that this is enough to give the US veto power over decisions requiring an 85

To the reader

Have the quotas described here changed since the writing of this book? Find out by going to the IMF website, www.imf.org, and looking up "voting power."

percent majority, such as changing quotas – hence influence – at the Fund.

Each member of the IMF has one representative governor (and one alternate) who sits on the Board of Governors and officially controls the member's votes.[14] The country representative is typically the finance minister or the head of the central bank. For example, the United States Governor is the Secretary of the Treasury (currently Henry Paulson) and the alternate is the Chairman of the Federal Reserve Board (currently Ben Bernanke). All of the power of the IMF comes from the Board of Governors. But the body typically meets only once a year, so most member countries are not directly involved in the day to day operations of the Fund. Instead, the Board of Governors delegates most of the decision-making authority to a smaller Executive Board, consisting of 24 "Directors."

The Directors of the Executive Board are appointed or elected by the Board of Governors at intervals of two years. The five members of the IMF with the largest quotas automatically get to appoint a Director to the Executive Board, and an additional one or two members may be allowed to appoint a Director if its currency is in particularly high demand.[15] Currently, the appointed Directors come from the United States, Japan, Germany, France, and the United Kingdom – but over time this group has changed:

- From 1946 to 1958, the appointed Directors were from the United States, the United Kingdom, *China*, France and *India*.
- In 1959 and 1960, a sixth Director was appointed by *Canada*.
- From 1961 to 1968, the appointed Directors were from the United States, the United Kingdom, France, Germany, and *India*.
- From 1969 to 1970, a sixth Director was appointed by *Italy*.
- Finally, starting in 1971, the top five members that appoint Directors today emerged, as Japan joined the United States, the United Kingdom, France, and Germany. *India* was able to appoint a sixth Director in 1971 and 1972, and *Saudi Arabia* was able to appoint a sixth Director from 1979 to 1992. Otherwise the top five have remained the same for over 30 years.

The members that get to appoint Directors are the most powerful at the Fund because they have the largest quotas and their currencies are in the highest demand by other countries. So, to an extent, the lists of countries in the above chronology reveal which countries had the most international economic importance. It is interesting to note the variation with appointed directors from Canada, China, India, Italy and

---

To the reader

Has the list of appointed directors changed since the writing of this book? Find out by going to the IMF website, www.imf.org, and looking up "Executive Directors."

Saudi Arabia in the early years of the Fund, followed by the long present static period.

The remaining Directors of the Executive Board are elected by the other members of the IMF. The Articles of Agreement allow for some discretion as to the precise number of elected Directors – these days there are 19. A few elected Directors represent just one economically powerful member with a large enough share of the votes, like Saudi Arabia, China, and Russia presently have. Most of the elected Directors, however, represent many members with small vote shares. To take an outstanding example, the Director from Equatorial Guinea currently represents his own country as well as twenty-three others.[16] Groups of countries seem to coalesce regionally or linguistically in their election of Directors, but there is no rule on this. There have been some non-obvious groupings throughout the history of the Fund.[17] Presently, for example, the Swiss Director represents Switzerland and Tajikistan as well as six other countries.[18] For decisions that the Executive Board votes on, each Director controls the sum total votes of the members he (they are almost all men) represents. The Director from Equatorial Guinea – even with the votes of 24 countries behind him – controls only 1.4 percent of the vote share on the Executive Board, while the US has the same share as on the Board of Governors, 17.08 percent.

While US power dwarfs other countries, some students are nevertheless surprised to learn that the US control of votes is a far cry from a majority. Even the cumulative vote share of the G-7[19] amounts to only 46.08 percent of the total. Yet, it is interesting to note that while the IMF explicitly refers to vote share as "voting power," students of political science know that vote *share* is often not equivalent to voting *power*. To see this, suppose there are 3 actors, one with 3 votes and two with one vote. The "vote share" of the actor with 3 out of the total 5 votes may only be 60 percent, but for decisions requiring a majority of votes, this actor is really a dictator with 100 percent of "voting power." In a 1954 article published in the *American Political Science Review*, L. S. Shapley and Martin Shubik – who defined "voting power" as the frequency with which an actor's votes are pivotal in making, breaking and blocking majority coalitions – showed that with as little as 40 percent of voting shares, an actor can effectively exercise 60 percent of voting power. In this vein, one can argue that if the largest five members – the US, Japan, Germany, France, and the UK – vote as a block, they control a majority of the voting power at the IMF.[20]

But perhaps all of this discussion of voting at the IMF is really just a red herring. According to a pamphlet published by the External Relations Department of the IMF,

> the executive board rarely makes its decisions on the basis of formal voting, but relies on the formation of consensus among its members, a practice that minimizes confrontation on sensitive issues and promotes agreement on the decisions ultimately taken.[21]

In pursuit of such "consensus," the Executive Board meets several times each week and appoints a Managing Director of the IMF for renewable five-year terms. By convention, the Managing Director of the IMF has always been a European (by contrast, the head of the World Bank is traditionally from the US). The Managing Director is much like the chief executive officer of a company. He (they have all

Box 1.4 IMF Managing Directors

Managing Director	From	Start date	End date
Camille Gutt	Belgium	May 6, 1946	May 5, 1951
Ivar Rooth	Sweden	August 3, 1951	October 3, 1956
Per Jacobsson	Sweden	November 21, 1956	May 5, 1963
Pierre-Paul Schweitzer	France	September 1, 1963	August 31, 1973
H. Johannes Witteveen	The Netherlands	September 1, 1973	June 16, 1978
Jacques de Larosière	France	June 17, 1978	January 15, 1987
Michel Camdessus	France	January 16, 1987	February 14, 2000
Horst Köhler	Germany	May 1, 2000	March 4, 2004
Rodrigo de Rato	Spain	June 7, 2004	present

To the reader

Is de Rato still in office? Find out by going to the IMF website, www.imf.org, and looking up "Managing Directors."

been men) is the chairman of the Executive Board and sits atop the IMF's bureaucratic hierarchy, assisted by the First Deputy Managing Director and two Deputy Managing Directors.

Beyond this, the IMF breaks down into various departments responsible for different tasks. For example, there are five area departments heading IMF operations in Africa, Asia and the Pacific, Europe, the Middle East and Central Asia, and the Western Hemisphere. The

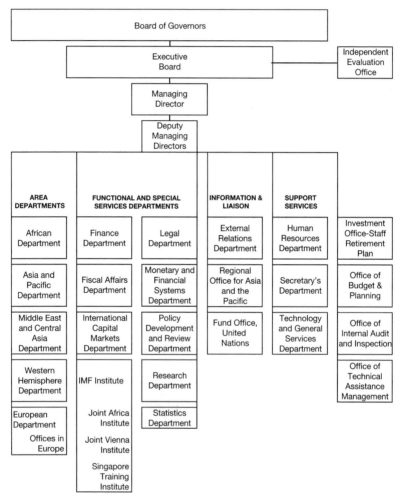

Figure 1.3 IMF organization chart.

Source: As of November 2003, adapted from www.imf.org.

vast majority of IMF departments are directly under the authority of the Managing Director and his Deputy Directors, as shown in Figure 1.3.

Outside of the regular hierarchy of the IMF is the Independent Evaluation Office (IEO), which reports directly to the Executive Board. As Chapter 6 discusses, the IEO was founded as a recent reform of the IMF. The purpose of the IEO is to provide objective evaluations of Fund operations. As Chapter 4 shows, one reason for such evaluations is that the success of IMF programs has been less than obvious, and IMF policies are not uncontroversial.

This brings back the question of how decisions are made at the Fund: if the IMF and the programs it sponsors are controversial, how can the Executive Board operate by "consensus," as described above? Some political scientists suspect that a system that relies on "the formation of consensus" to "minimize confrontation" really allows a powerful country like the United States to exercise more power than its official vote share. J. Lawrence Broz and Michael Brewster Hawes, political scientists at the University of California, San Diego, note that small members may fear retaliation from the US for taking positions the US opposes.[22]

Yet, the "sense of the meeting" approach apparently came about in the early years of the Fund (around 1953–1954) as a means for the US Executive Director "to exercise his power without convincing the rest of the Directors that discussion was futile because the US view would prevail."[23] The result was much lengthier discussions searching for common ground. Some say that this method of consensus building allows small countries the opportunity to have increased influence because a carefully turned phrase may persuade powerful members.

Nevertheless, the Managing Director or First Deputy Managing Director keeps track of straw polls gathered through discussions of where the majority lies so that even though official votes are rarely taken, the "majority will" presumably rules.[24] Still, it is not obvious how votes translate into power at the IMF. Maybe the "consensus" approach gives powerful members more say on issues that they care most about, but allows more say to smaller members on less salient issues. For now, let us remain agnostic, as Chapter 2 explores in more depth the question of who controls the IMF.

The important point is that while the IMF has a complicated accounting system for assigning votes, actual voting is not the norm. The fact that decision-making at the IMF appears opaque to outsiders disturbs many who are concerned with the IMF practice of imposing policy conditions in return for IMF loans – the IMF practice of conditionality.

Conditionality background

With an understanding of who the IMF is and where its resources come from, let us return to conditionality. Recall that as an international lender, the IMF provides loans of foreign currency to countries in a balance of payments crisis or to countries that the IMF deems – for whatever reason – to have a shortfall in foreign reserves.[25] The guidelines for providing these loans are spelled out in Article V of the IMF Articles of Agreement, which states that a member may request an IMF loan when it has a need "because of its balance of payments or its reserve position or developments in its reserves."

IMF loans can thus be thought of as a form of insurance against the risk of a balance of payments crisis. Like most forms of insurance, however, this introduces the possibility of something economists call "moral hazard."

Moral hazard rears its head whenever individuals who have insured themselves against a risk behave more recklessly than they would without insurance. Imagine, for example, how people might drive and park their cars if every little ding and dent were repaired and paid for by their insurance companies. If the driver did not bear a cost for repairing the vehicle, he would have less incentive to be careful. Of course, insurance companies, well aware of moral hazard, have several mechanisms to counteract it, such as high deductibles, rewards for clean driving records, and penalties for records of accidents. There are many ways of dealing with moral hazard. The IMF answer is conditionality.

How does conditionality work to fend off moral hazard? If governments know they can get a loan of foreign currency from the IMF whenever they enter into an economic crisis, they may have less incentive to avoid the crisis in the first place (individual investors may also behave more recklessly if they expect a country to be bailed out of any economic crisis). Thus, when the IMF deems that a country's need for a loan is the result of *bad economic policies*, the IMF attaches policy conditions to the loan. These policy conditions are intended to correct the bad policies and ultimately resolve the economic crisis. As stated in the Articles of Agreement (Article V, Section 3(a)):

> The Fund ... may adopt special policies for special balance of payments problems, that will assist members to solve their balance of payments problems in a manner consistent with the provisions of this Agreement and that will establish adequate safeguards for the temporary use of the general resources of the Fund.

Box 1.5 Loans or purchases?

It is conventional in the media, in scholarly work, and even at the IMF itself to refer to the foreign currency the IMF provides to countries as "loans" (this is the term used in this book too). Technically, however, IMF "loans" are usually "purchases" of foreign currency. As stated in the Articles of Agreement (Article V, Section 3(b)), a member of the IMF is "entitled to *purchase* the currencies of other members from the Fund in exchange for an equivalent amount of its own currency" (emphasis added).

If a developing country like Ghana, for example, requires 100 million euros to pay off a foreign debt, the Ghanaian government purchases the euros from the IMF with the equivalent amount of its national currency, the cedi. Subsequently, the Ghanaian government is required (usually over a period of no more than five years) to buy back (or "repurchase") the cedis with euros. Eventually, the amount of euros that were originally purchased is paid back, and a premium is charged so that interest is effectively included in the repurchase (the effective interest rate charged is equivalent to what the IMF deems as the market rate). For all intents and purposes, this is equivalent to a loan, which is why the word is so commonly used, but in the official documents and statements of the IMF, one will usually find the words "purchase" and "repurchase."

The arrangement of providing a loan contingent upon policy conditions is known as "conditionality," a concept laden with controversy – indeed, the center of IMF controversy.

The controversy actually dates back to the earliest days of the IMF. When Harry Dexter White returned to Washington to present the Bretton Woods Agreement on the IMF, members of the US Congress questioned whether IMF lending would become an unlimited liability. Would lending continuously subsidize growing balance of payments deficits? White assured questioners that IMF lending would be *conditioned* on countries following policies to correct their balance of payments problems. Yet, at the same time, John Maynard Keynes was presenting a different vision of the IMF to the members of the British Parliament, who feared that IMF lending would entail policy conditions that would impinge upon national sovereignty. Keynes assured them that IMF policy advice would be limited, and that domestic policies would be "immune from criticism by the fund."[26] Yet Keynes was well-aware of US wishes. He noted that the US wanted an institution "with wide discretionary and policing powers."[27] Nevertheless, he went on to write that the US representatives had been persuaded "of the undesirability of starting off by giving so much authority to an untried institution."[28] Keynes' hope for the IMF – that domestic policies would not be criticized – did not come to fruition. Domestic politics are at the heart of every IMF arrangement.[29]

Conditionality was not explicitly incorporated by the IMF until the Articles of Agreement were amended in 1968.[30] Yet, even before this amendment, conditionality was implicit in the IMF mandate and put into practice from the beginning, as White had assured the US Congress. For example, after the IMF made its first loan to France in 1947, the IMF made France ineligible to use Fund resources in 1948 because the IMF did not approve of the French exchange rate policies.[31] The codification of conditionality actually began as early as 1952, when the IMF introduced "Stand-by Arrangements." An Executive Board Decision on February 13 of that year announced that Fund resources should be used to help members provided "the policies the members will pursue will be adequate to overcome the problem."[32] Over the years since these early decisions, conditionality has evolved considerably, notably following major crises the IMF has faced.

Conditionality: from "macro" to "micro" to "ownership"

The first IMF arrangement with a developing country, Peru in 1954, was intended to help Peru adjust its exchange rate in the face of declining reserves.[33] The Peruvian government promised to lower domestic consumption by "stabilizing the country's fiscal position, which involved a slowing down of some investment projects already under way and the postponement of additional investment expenditures" (IMF Annual Report 1954: 90–1). Over time, the policy conditions contained in IMF arrangements became more and more specific. Sociologist Sarah Babb of Boston College and economist Ariel Buira of the G-24 Secretariat, report that the Stand-by Arrangements with Peru in 1954, 1963, and 1993 were two, six, and thirteen pages in length, respectively. The 1954 program, described above was very general. The 1963 arrangement contained more specific conditions – fiscal and monetary targets. The 1993 agreement not only included fiscal and monetary targets, but also targets for international reserves, limitations of foreign debt, a prohibition against import restrictions, further provisions for trade liberalization, as well as conditions calling for privatization and the deregulation of labor laws.[34]

In the early years, when conditions were fewer in number and less detailed, the IMF practiced what has come to be called "macro-conditionality." Usually the policy conditions included (1) reducing the government budget deficit, by cutting spending and raising taxes, (2) reducing the money supply, by raising central bank interest rates and placing ceilings on credit creation, and (3) sometimes the devaluation of the national currency.[35]

The IMF still typically includes these conditions because it views balance of payments problems as problems of excess "demand" – there is too much consumption of imported goods. IMF policies are intended to lower this consumption, especially consumption in the public sector. This is why fiscal conditions are imposed, where IMF arrangements require governments to lower public expenditures and raise taxes to lower the fiscal deficit. Tight monetary policy – where governments raise interest rates, reduced credit creation, and placed limits on public borrowing – reduces the money supply, which also lowers consumption. Sometimes the IMF prescribes devaluation of the national currency so that the price of imports rises while the price of exports drops. This is intended to make it easier for countries to earn foreign exchange through increased exports and reduces the purchase of imports.

Note that these policies are broad. Targets for IMF programs could be achieved through various specific policy means. Fiscal deficits, for example, could be reduced by cutting inefficient public expenditures or by cutting valuable public investment. "Macro-conditionality," left a lot of room for domestic politics to play a role in how governments achieved the macro-economic targets of IMF arrangements.

Nevertheless, macro-conditionality impinged on national sovereignty. Addressing this in a review of conditionality during the late 1970s, the IMF stated that "the Fund will pay due regard to the domestic social and political objectives, the economic priorities, and the circumstances of members."[36] The IMF also, however, sought to extend the scope of conditionality, encouraging countries to turn to the IMF early on before a balance of payments problem becomes too severe. It even stated that some prior actions or "pre-conditions" might be required of some governments before a Stand-by Arrangement can be put in place.[37]

Soon after these guidelines were published, the Latin American Debt Crisis of the early 1980s ensued. The fact that these particular developing countries faced such a deep and widespread crisis was a striking problem for the IMF. After all, countries of this region had participated in more IMF programs than any other in the world.

Most Latin American countries entered into their first IMF arrangement during the 1950s. By 1965 *every* Latin American country had participated – and most of them on a repeating basis. Why did Latin America face the debt crisis after extensive participation in IMF programs? Were IMF policies the wrong ones? The IMF argued not. It was instead argued that programs had not gone deep enough. The macro-conditions had failed to address fundamental weaknesses in developing countries' economies.

Structural adjustment was deemed necessary. The problem with imposing broad conditions was that countries could comply with the letter of the program without complying with the spirit. It was not only important that balance was restored to an economy but also *how* balance was restored. If the fundamental structure of a country's economy was not addressed, the balance of payments problem would return.

Thus, the IMF began to impose more specific and deeper policies on countries. For example, rather than simply calling for a reduction of the fiscal deficit, the IMF called for *privatization* and *deregulation*. Privatization involves transferring the ownership of national assets to the private sector, where free markets would bring about greater efficiency. Deregulation involves removing restrictions on businesses and prices, allowing the forces of markets to operate, which is desirable if the decentralized decisions of individuals bring about greater efficiency than the actions of the central authority. Other structural changes might involve fundamental changes to taxation policies, labor market policies, or national pension programs. Structural conditions sometimes even involve reducing barriers to trade, such as tariffs on imports or subsidies to exports.

In the 1990s, the term "micro-conditionality" began to be used to describe the level of detail of IMF program conditions. The overall number of conditions included in agreements exploded. Jacques Polak, former IMF Director of Research and member of the IMF Executive Board, reports that the average number of conditions went from below six in the late 1960s/early 1970s, to seven in the late 1970s/early 1980s, to over nine in the late 1980s.[38] Then, as economist Graham Bird – the Director of the Surrey Centre for International Economic Studies and one of the most widely published scholars on the IMF – describes, the average number of conditions per IMF arrangement went up to 9.9 in 1993, 10.5 in 1994, 11.0 in 1995, 13.0 in 1996, and 16 in 1997.[39]

Micro-conditionality came under attack, however, in the aftermath of the East Asian financial crisis, which began in Thailand in 1997, and soon spread to Indonesia, South Korea, the Philippines, Hong Kong, and Malaysia, followed by Russia and Brazil. Subsequently,

Argentina experienced a catastrophic collapse of its economy in 2001.[40] Many criticized how the IMF handled the East Asian financial crisis, and IMF micro-conditionality came under attack. There are many critiques of specific policies – too many to list. A basic consensus that came about, however, was that IMF conditionality had gone too far in the opposite direction of macro-conditionality. Micro-conditionality was too detailed.[41]

In response to failures in so many important countries, the IMF proposed a new approach to conditionality: "ownership." Again, the IMF argued that its overall approach to economic crises was correct – the problem continued to be that countries failed in some way to implement the program. Officials and staff at the IMF reasoned that the problem was a lack of commitment on the part of participating countries. As the IMF describes on its webpage,[42] "During 2000–2001, the IMF worked to streamline its conditionality – making it more sharply focused on macroeconomic and financial sector policies, less intrusive into countries' policy choices, more conducive to country *ownership* of policy programs, and thus more effective" [emphasis added].

It should be noted that this new approach to IMF conditionality is not entirely new. It echoes the guideline published in 1979, cited above, calling for due regard to domestic social and political objectives and domestic economic priorities. Moreover, the IMF has not changed its fundamental approach to economic problems – reducing excess demand.

But the IMF has promised a new approach to the negotiation and design of programs. A surprising statement included in a report by the IMF Policy Development and Review Department notes that beyond negotiations with a country's financial authorities the Fund can also play a role in promoting ownership "by holding substantive discussions with other groups, including other ministries, trade unions, industry representatives, and local non-governmental organizations, especially at a stage at which the design of the program is still under consideration."[43]

It is too soon to tell whether the "ownership" approach to conditionality will evidence any change in program outcomes, but it is interesting to note the solution to IMF program failures of the 1970s was *increasing* conditionality in the 1980s and 1990s, and the solution to IMF program failures in the 1990s is *reducing* conditionality in the new century.

Lending facilities

The vast majority of IMF lending is conditioned, but there are some loans with no strings attached. The IMF recognizes that sometimes a country's need for a loan is not the result of reckless bad economic policy, but rather just bad luck. In these cases, moral hazard is not a problem, and the IMF can provide loans without policy conditions.

How does the IMF determine if need is due to bad policy or bad luck? The rule of thumb is somewhat arbitrary. If a country requests a small loan – 25 percent or less of its quota – the loan is provided without conditions. The rationale behind this rule is that members must provide the first 25 percent of their quotas in a hard currency – such as the dollar, the yen, the pound or the euro. Thus, when a government borrows up to 25 percent of its quota, the loan is really just drawing back its own hard currency already held on deposit at the IMF. Nevertheless, there is no theory behind why 25 percent is the appropriate cut-off. The IMF reviews quotas only every five years, and they rarely change even though the exposure of developing countries to international markets is growing dramatically. Considering how controversial conditionality is, it is surprising that this cut-off rule is rarely discussed or debated.[44]

In addition to the first 25 percent of the quota being condition-free, the IMF has opened other "lending facilities" free of conditions because the need for these loans is deemed to be the result of bad luck. For example, the IMF established the Compensatory Financing Facility in 1963 to provide loans to developing countries dependent upon primary commodity exports when the prices of these commodities decline sharply. Since these loans were intended to be truly temporary and not due to bad policy, conditionality was set very low for this facility.[45] Another similar facility is the Oil Facility, which the IMF opened in the early 1970s – when the price of oil quadrupled – to finance the oil-related deficits of oil-importing developing countries.

Sometimes governments in need of an IMF loan go to great lengths to avoid IMF conditions. Take, for example, Tanzania in 1974. With the rise in world oil prices, this fuel-importing country entered into a balance of payments crisis. President Julius Nyerere borrowed from the IMF exactly 25 percent of Tanzania's quota, and subsequently obtained two consecutive loans from the unconditioned Oil Facility. In sum, Nyerere obtained loans of nearly 50 percent of Tanzania's quota (about 20 million SDR) and avoided conditionality. He did this both because he opposed the policy conditions that the IMF proposed were necessary for Tanzania, and because he opposed what he saw as an international organization infringing upon national sovereignty.

As another example, consider Nigeria in 1982. With the drop in world oil prices, this oil-exporting country entered into a balance of payments crisis and turned to the IMF. President Alhaji Shehu Shagari withdrew a loan of 25 percent of his country's quota, followed by an Oil Facility loan. Shagari also entered into negotiations for a conditioned IMF arrangement, but could not come to an agreement over the appropriate policy conditions. In particular, the IMF insisted that the national currency, the naira, be devalued, but the Nigerian president could not take this step – he faced elections and devaluation was politically risky.[46]

Eventually, Tanzania and Nigeria – and nearly every other developing country–succumbed to the need to accept IMF conditionality. So, what are the *conditioned* IMF lending facilities? And what happens when a country enters into an arrangement to borrow under one of these facilities?

Box 1.6 IMF program virgins

Most countries in the world have participated in an IMF arrangement, and for most developing countries, this participation has been extensive. But there is a substantial number of countries that have never participated in an IMF program. How have these countries avoided the IMF?

For some, the reasons are deeply political, and they are not even members of the IMF (e.g. North Korea). The majority on the list, however, are members, but still have not participated. Their reasons are not obvious.

Resource rich countries such as the oil-exporting states of the Middle East and diamond-exporting Botswana have never turned to the IMF for a conditioned loan because their natural resources have generated enough foreign exchange that they have never needed an IMF loan. But being resource rich does not explain all of the patterns of participation. Will Botswana continue without the IMF if it depends too heavily on diamonds? The question of national sovereignty may play a role here even if economic problems develop (see Chapter 3). Why has resource-rich Angola avoided the IMF while the resource-rich Democratic Republic of Congo (formerly Zaire) had an extensive history of IMF program participation? Cold War politics may tell part of this story (see Chapter 2).

Some small island countries in the Caribbean and the Pacific have also avoided the IMF. Why some island countries have prospered on their own and been able to avoid the IMF while others have not is an open question. The former British colonies of Dominica and Grenada had extensive IMF programs in the 1980s while neighboring St. Lucia, also a former British colony, never did.

Table 1.1 Countries that have never participated in a conditioned IMF arrangment (1945–2004)

Africa		Asia	
Country	*IMF membership*	*Country*	*IMF membership*
Angola	1989 –	Bhutan	1981 –
Botswana	1968 –	Brunei	1995 –
Eritrea	1994 –	Korea, North	–
Libya	1958 –	Malaysia	1958 –
Namibia	1990 –	Maldive Islands	1978 –
Seychelles	1977 –	Singapore	1966 –
Swaziland	1969 –	Taiwan	1949 – 1980

The Americas		Europe	
Country	*IMF membership*	*Country*	*IMF membership*
Antigua and Barbuda	1982 –	Andorra	–
Bahamas	1973 –	Austria	1948 –
Canada	1945 –	Denmark	1946 –
Saint Kitts and Nevis	1984 –	East Germany*	–
Saint Lucia	1979 –	Germany	1952 –
Saint Vincent	1979 –	Greece	1945 –
Suriname	1978 –	Ireland	1957 –
		Liechtenstein	–
		Luxembourg	1945 –

Middle East			
Country	*IMF membership*	Malta	1968 –
Bahrain	1972 –	Norway	1945 –
Iraq	1945 –	San Marino	1992 –
Kuwait	1962 –	Slovenia	1992 –
Lebanon	1947 –	Sweden	1951 –
Oman	1971 –	Switzerland	1992 –
Qatar	1972 –	USSR**	–
Saudi Arabia	1957 –		

		Pacific Islands	
Turkmenistan	1992 –	*Country*	*IMF membership*
United Arab Emirates	1972 –	Kiribati	1986 –
		Marshall Islands	1992 –
Yemen PDR (South)*	1969 – 1990	Micronesia	1993 –
		Nauru	–
Yemen Arab Rep.*	1970 – 1990	Palau	1997 –
		Tonga	1985 –
		Vanuatu	1981 –

Notes: * Country ceased to exist as an independent state in 1990.
          ** Country ceased to exist in 1991.

To the reader

This list was composed as of January 2005 – have any of the countries on the list finally turned to the IMF for a conditioned loan? Find out by going to the IMF website, www.imf.org, and looking up specific countries under "Country Info." Interested in seeing the other countries – those that have participated in IMF programs? The data set used for this book is available at my web page: http://pantheon.yale.edu~jrv9.

Historically, there have been four main conditioned lending facilities (although two of them are no longer in use, and one of them has changed names).[47] IMF programs – alternatively called IMF agreements, but officially called "IMF arrangements" – from these four facilities have the same basic goals: stabilize the economy and set the stage for renewed prosperity.

The facilities differ in the interest rates charged on the loans – one of them provides "concessional" loans at an interest rate below the market rate (this "market rate" is somewhat controversial itself, since it probably does not apply to developing countries in need of IMF assistance). Supposedly, the facilities also differ in their intended time horizons. Since most arrangements are entered into consecutively, however, the time horizon for programs turns out to be arbitrary, even though the designers of IMF programs may have specific time-frames in mind at the outset of programs. The broad objectives of the facilities are the same: to first stabilize the country's economy and then set the stage for recovery and new prosperity.

The oldest and historically most used facility is the one that was mentioned above: "stand-by." These arrangements were so named because a line of credit is set aside to "stand by" in case the participating country requires a loan. Stand-by Arrangements (or SBAs) are intended to last one to two years, and countries can draw designated amounts at designated intervals – subject to reviews of compliance with the policy conditions – to deal with temporary balance of payments problems.

The first SBA transaction was announced May 12, 1952: "Finland might purchase up to $5 million from the Fund at any time during the next six months."[48] In fact, this agreement was not actually signed until January 1953, and in the interim the first agreement was signed with Belgium on June 19, 1952.[49] After Belgium and Finland, other European countries entered into SBAs: France (1956), United Kingdom (1956), the Netherlands (1957), and Spain (1959). To the extent that the IMF was involved in Western Europe, the organization was playing the role it was originally intended to play. But the IMF did not conduct many bailouts of industrialized countries.

This is not to say that developed countries never used the IMF. Japan participated in a one-year SBA starting January 19, 1962, and then entered into another one-year arrangement on March 11, 1964. Similarly, the United States entered into consecutive one-year SBAs on July 22, 1963 and 1964. The United Kingdom continued participating in SBAs until the 1970s, with its last arrangement expiring January 2, 1979. The last Western European countries to participate in SBAs were Spain (February 6, 1978 – February 5, 1979) and Portugal (October 7, 1983 – February 28, 1985).

In the meantime, Latin American countries were also entering into SBAs: Peru (1954), Mexico (1954), Bolivia (1956), Chile (1956), Cuba (1956), Nicaragua (1956), Colombia (1957), Honduras (1957), Paraguay (1957), Argentina (1958), Brazil (1958), El Salvador (1958), Haiti (1958), and the Dominican Republic (1959). Even countries in Asia and Africa entered SBAs as early as the 1950s: Iran (1956), India (1957), Pakistan (1958), South Africa (1958), and Morocco (1959). As early as 1960, SBA participation was *worldwide*, and once a developing country entered into one IMF arrangement, it was likely to enter into another … and another.

"Recidivism," as it has been called in the IMF scholarly literature, is common. Arrangements lasting more than six months became the norm early on. The first arrangement with Peru began February 18, 1954, and expired February 17, 1958 – a *four year* arrangement. Time limits of one to two years appear meaningless when looking at the broad patterns of participation. The average stint of participation is about five years. Once a country leaves such a stint, it is typical for it to return again after another five years. Some cases are extreme. South Korea spent 13 years under consecutive agreements from 1965 to 1977; Zaire spent 14 years straight (1976–89); Liberia spent 15 years (1963–77). Peru participated in consecutive agreements from 1954 to 1971 (18 years) followed by several other stints of participation: 1977–1980, 1982–1985, 1993–2004. Panama participated from 1968 to 1987 (20 years of consecutive agreements) and returned to participate from 1992 to 2002. Haiti, after a stint of seven years (1961 to 1967), entered into agreements again from 1970 to 1989, and again from 1995 to 1999. The Philippines has the most extensive participation: 1962–1969, 1971–1981, 1983–2000.

Even early on, IMF Staff and Officials recognized that the "temporary" problems SBAs were intended to address lasted longer than two years. In 1963, the IMF initiated the Extended Fund Facility (EFF), under which programs were expected to last three to four years. These time limits still appeared to be arbitrary, however, as EFFs were often preceded or followed by SBAs. The policy conditions as well as the goals of the SBAs and the EFFs were basically the same.

After the Latin American Debt Crisis of the early 1980s, the IMF initiated two new lending facilities in 1986 and 1987: the Structural Adjustment Facility (SAF) and the Enhanced Structural Adjustment Facility (ESAF). These facilities, like the EFF, were intended to last longer than SBAs, and they were supposed to prescribe structural conditions to fundamentally adjust developing countries' economies. Furthermore, the ESAF provided loans at discounted – or "concessional" – interest rates and was intended to target only the poorest countries in the world. While the IMF created these two new facilities explicitly to address the new emphasis on structural adjustment discussed above, SBA and EFF programs also began to require structural conditions.

Finally, as one of the changes undertaken by the IMF in the aftermath of the aforementioned East Asian crisis, the IMF changed the name of the ESAF facility to the Poverty Reduction and Growth Facility (PRGF). The goals of the facility did not change, but this facility in particular was to emphasize the new focus on country "ownership" of IMF economic reform programs. As discussed above, the hope is to engender greater government accountability.

Today, the only two conditioned facilities in use are the SBA and the PRGF. The 2005 IMF Annual Report details that the last SAF arrangement to be approved was in 1996, the last EFF arrangement was approved in 2003. Historically, SBAs account for more than 75 percent of all IMF programs ever approved by the IMF, but in the new century PRGF programs have begun to outpace SBAs. The 2005 IMF Annual Report notes that there were eight new PRFG arrangements approved in 2005, but only six new SBAs.[50]

The actual arrangement

So what exactly does an IMF arrangement look like and how does a country enter into one? IMF arrangements are a strange breed of international agreement. Legally, in fact, they are not international "agreements" at all! The government and the IMF do not exchange signatures; they are not registered with the United Nations; and if the government fails to live up to promises made, there is no breach of international law. So, in a legal sense, IMF arrangements are not international agreements.

This is no accident. As Joseph Gold, former Director of the IMF Legal Department, explains, the IMF never intended Stand-by Arrangements to be legally binding international agreements.[51] To make this clear to outside observers, the IMF has stated this in various ways throughout its history. For example, the Executive Board Decision of 2 March 1979 states: "Stand-by Arrangements are not international agreements and therefore language having a contractual connotation will be avoided … "[52]

In many countries, legally binding international *agreements* must be ratified domestically before they go into force. As Gold explains, this is not the case with IMF arrangements: "Members do not submit stand-by arrangements to the domestic procedures that are followed for entry into treaties or international agreements."[53] As far as the IMF is concerned, a domestic ratification process is not required.

If there is no exchange of signatures, how does a country actually enter into an IMF arrangement? In a nutshell, it goes something like this: a letter detailing the arrangement – the loan and the policy conditions – is sent from the executive branch of the government to the IMF Managing Director. The Managing Director presents the arrangement, as detailed in the letter and any supporting documents cited in the letter, to the IMF Executive Board, and if the Executive Board approves, the first installment of the loan is disbursed and the country goes under the IMF arrangement. That is all.

To be more specific, IMF arrangements are spelled out in something called a "Letter of Intent" (LOI). The LOI describes the policies that a government *intends* to pursue in return for financial support from the IMF. This letter is addressed to the IMF Managing Director and is usually signed by the country's finance minister, although it may also be signed by the president of the central bank, or even the prime minister or president. The signatory is not necessarily the author, however. The LOI is drafted behind closed doors by the IMF staff visiting the country and country officials. Since the negotiations are private, no one knows for certain, but it has been routinely claimed that the Letters of Intent are often drafted entirely by IMF staff. The new focus on country "ownership" is something the IMF has initiated to change this. The IMF has also become concerned with "transparency," making more information about the details of arrangements publicly available. Historically, the LOIs were kept secret for many years before being made available at the IMF archives in Washington, DC. Since 1999, however, nearly all LOIs have been posted, at least in part, on the IMF website.

Note that the IMF prefers not to get directly involved in the domestic politics of program countries. So it works exclusively with the part of government that the IMF deems the "proper authority" over the economy – usually the finance ministry and/or the central bank. Yet the finance ministry may not have power over certain areas of the economy, such as the budget deficit. There may be a national legislature involved in the government budgeting process. There may be local governments with the power to tax and spend. So LOI often includes promises in policy areas over which the finance ministry has little or no authority. This is an issue that both Chapters 3 and 5 address.

When do IMF arrangements go into effect? Once drafted, the IMF Managing Director presents the LOI to the Executive Board. If the Board approves, the arrangement begins, and the country embarks on its participation in the IMF program: the IMF makes the first loan disbursement, and monitoring of compliance with policy conditions begins. As noted at the beginning of the chapter, the lives of billions have been affected by participation in these arrangements through both the IMF loan and the policy conditions attached to the loan. The rest of the book explores why countries participate and with what effects.

Box 1.7 An IMF Letter of Intent

Below are excerpts from the 2001 Pakistan Letter of Intent. This letter, along with many others published since the end of the 1990s, is available under "Country Info" at the IMF website, www.imf.org.[54]

Pakistan – Letter of Intent,
Memorandum of Economic and Financial Policies,
Technical Memorandum of Understanding

November 22, 2001

Dear [Managing Director] Mr. Köhler,

The government of Pakistan has adopted an economic reform program for 2001–4, which aims to increase sustainable growth and strengthen basic social services as the central pillars of its poverty reduction strategy. To reach these goals, the government is determined to pursue sound macroeconomic policies, create the conditions for vibrant private sector development, and strengthen efforts on basic education and health as well as social safety nets. The details of the program are set out in the attached Memorandum on Economic and Financial Policies (MEFP) … In support of this program, we request a three-year arrangement under the Poverty Reduction and Growth Facility (PRGF) in an amount equivalent to SDR 1,033.7 million (100 percent of quota)...

Sincerely yours,

Shaukat Aziz
*Minister of Finance
and Economic*

Ishrat Husain
*Governor,
State Bank of Pakistan*

Note that the program is set to last three years. At the time of this arrangement, however, Pakistan was just finishing another arrangement. Indeed, Pakistan had participated in consecutive IMF arrangements since 1993 and before that in: 1958–59, 1965–66, 1968–69, 1972–75, 1977–78, 1980–83, and 1988–91. Not surprisingly, Pakistan entered a new arrangement after this one, issuing a new Letter of Intent right on schedule: November 12, 2004.

Following the introduction, the letter proceeds to the "Memorandum of Economic and Financial Policies" and the "Technical Memorandum of Understanding" which describe the specific policies conditions Pakistan promises to follow. First, the letter addresses poverty. In the past, explicit conditions concerning poverty were not typically included in IMF agreements. This represents a change from earlier eras. The Fund's prior view on this was that stabilization policies would set the stage to alleviate poverty. Now, explicit conditions on education and health care for the poor are included. Note, however, that the level of growth required to achieve the objectives may be unrealistic. To implement a full poverty reduction strategy, the World Bank estimates that Pakistan will have to aim for an economic growth rate of 7 to 8 per cent for at least ten years:

The government is strongly committed to undertaking specific actions to reduce the burden of poverty affecting the people of Pakistan. We believe that growth and the related income-generating opportunities are essential in reducing poverty over time, but we also know that in a context where about one-third of the population is poor, it is not possible to wait for the benefit of growth to trickle down and address the poverty issue. Policies to improve access to basic services such as primary education, preventive health care and population and welfare services, and measures that increase efficiency in the delivery of public services will take center stage over the coming year ... To achieve those objectives, the government is committed to raising over time the resources allocated to programs deemed effective in supporting social development and responding to the poverty problem ...

The letter then addresses fiscal conditions, something that has commonly been included in IMF arrangements since the beginning. It is interesting to note that when Pakistan entered into a 3 year arrangement in 1997, the government committed to reducing the fiscal deficit from 7 percent of GDP to 4 percent by the year 2000. Although this target was not achieved, the outcome was close, as government the reduced the deficit to about 5 percent of GDP.

The structural reform agenda also includes commitments to improved monitoring and transparency in public finances, tax reform "gradually unifying corporate income tax rates towards 35 percent," and reforming the tax administration – the "cornerstone in the institutional reform agenda." In 2000, the government of Pakistan admitted that the previous administration had submitted false data.

Additional structural reform promises are made with respect to trade policy. Measures include a reduction of the maximum tariff to 25 percent. Regarding monetary policy, the letter asserts that it will remain "geared to keep inflation in check while supporting the targeted accumulation of international reserves."

There are also privatization conditions, promising "the sale of remaining public shares in Muslim Commercial Bank and Allied Bank and with the sale through the stock market of 5 percent of the capital of National Bank of Pakistan." The letter goes on to promise that the national telecommunication company will be brought to the point of sale in early 2002. Pension and civil service reform are also promised, as well as reforms to the financial sector and foreign exchange market. The level of detail is remarkable. Even the specific dates when various structural reforms should be achieved are included in a table attached to the letter.

The letter goes on to discuss program monitoring. Under Pakistan's prior Stand-by Arrangement, the government passed all 3 IMF reviews, obtaining each of the promised disbursements of credit on time. If the IMF deems that a government is not making sufficient progress complying with policy conditions, loan disbursements can be suspended, and arrangements can even be cancelled.

The new PRGF arrangement will involve quarterly reviews and disbursements. The period for the first year of the program is October 2001 – September 2002. The first review will be completed by end-March 2002 and will focus on the implementation of macro-economic policies, progress in tax administration reforms, and progress in monitoring fiscal expenditure, especially for social expenditures and outcomes. The second review will be completed by end-June 2002.

This arrangement was approved by the IMF Executive Board on December 6, 2001.

2   Who controls the IMF?

A country's influence at the IMF is supposed to come from the share of votes it controls, which is pegged to the country's economic size. Voting, however, is rare at the Fund. Rather, the Fund operates by consensus. While this consensus rule was adopted in the early years of the IMF to allow greater say to members beside the US, many believe that IMF "consensus" is nonetheless dominated by the United States. New evidence suggests that non-governmental actors, such as international financiers, also have an important voice in the shaping of IMF programs.

This chapter explores the question of who controls the IMF, looking at evidence of both US dominance and the influence of international financiers. Before turning to this evidence, however, the chapter begins with a different perspective: the view that the IMF has become an independent power unto itself.

A power unto itself?

The IMF claims the following:

> Many people view the IMF as an institution of great authority and independence ... Nothing could be further from the truth. Far from being dictated to by the IMF, the membership itself dictates to the IMF the policies it will follow. The chain of command runs clearly from the governments of member countries to the IMF and not vice versa.[1]

Is the IMF held entirely accountable by its membership, as this quotation asserts, or is accountability along the "chain of command" lax, allowing the IMF to pursue its own goals? Does the IMF hold any independent power?

It is certainly true that the ultimate authority of the IMF derives from its members. Yet, with IMF programs, the chain of command is a long one: the routine activities of the IMF are carried out by the IMF staff – typically, the staff negotiates the details of IMF arrangements, and they engage in routine surveillance of all members' economies. The staff reports to officials higher up in the bureaucratic chain of command. Atop the bureaucratic chain of command sits the Managing Director of the IMF. The Managing Director reports to the Executive Board, which meets several times a week. The Directors who serve on the Executive Board are either appointed or elected by the Board of Governors, which meets about once a year. Each Governor serving on the Board – typically a country's finance minister or central bank governor – is appointed by the government of the member country. The countries with the most votes on the Board of Governors are democracies, due to their economic size and importance. Thus, the governments appointing the most powerful IMF Governors are themselves elected by the voters of the member countries. So, in principle, the IMF derives its authority from the citizens of the world. Figure 2.1 draws out this chain of command.

Average citizens, however, do not appear to influence the IMF. The chain of command is long and circuitous, and at each link in the chain some degree of control is lost. One cannot take perfect control for granted. At any point in the chain of command, accountability can break down. Considering the chain of command as a whole, there are ample opportunities for accountability to fall apart.

Economist Roland Vaubel, of the University of Mannheim, Germany, has made the case that accountability problems at the IMF are so severe that the IMF pursues its own goals.[2] He argues that "international bureaucracies ... try to maximize their power in terms of budget size, staff and freedom of discretion and appreciate some leisure on the job."[3] It is easy for an outsider to make this accusation, but Vaubel substantiates the claim with some interesting evidence.

For one, Vaubel considers the size of the IMF staff, which has grown over time. He notes that this could be due to increasing volumes of international financial flows leading to a greater need for the IMF. But it could also be because the IMF seeks greater resources as an ends in itself. More staff means less work per individual. Thus, Vaubel analyzes the change in the IMF staff size over time. As possible explanatory factors, he includes economic variables accounting for the growth of international financial flows. He also includes an "accountability variable." The measure he uses to capture "accountability" is the percentage of votes controlled by the ten largest members of the IMF. The smaller

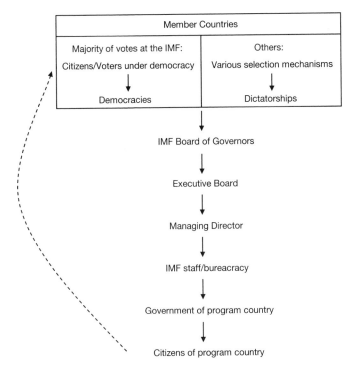

Figure 2.1 Chain of command from IMF members down to IMF program country.

the share of votes a member controls, the less influence a member has, and thus the smaller incentive the member has to monitor the activities of IMF officials and staff. As the number of IMF members has increased over time, the share of votes controlled by the ten largest members has decreased. In 1958 it was 76 percent, in 1985 it was 58 percent, and today it is about 54 percent. Vaubel reasons that if the percentage of votes controlled by the largest members declines, the overall level of monitoring declines because authority is dispersed. Interestingly, Vaubel finds a statistically significant correlation between his "accountability variable" and the size of the IMF staff – even after controlling for other economic factors. Indeed, he finds that the other variables do not explain as much as his accountability variable. Vaubel takes this as evidence that the increasing staff is partly the result of a bureaucracy taking advantage of weak monitoring by those supposedly in charge.

Vaubel also examines something he calls "hurry-up lending."[4] The IMF Articles of Agreement stipulate that quotas – from which the IMF gets its resources – must be reviewed at least every five years. Vaubel argues that there is less pressure to demonstrate a need for increased quotas immediately following a review of quota size because the next review is years away. But after three years, the next review is on the horizon, so the pace of IMF lending increases. Vaubel speculates that the IMF "hurries up" its lending activities as the next quota review approaches. Successful hurry-up lending allows the IMF to show a strong need for increased resources. Vaubel's analysis of data on the IMF's total use of its lending capacity reveals an interesting pattern supporting his hypothesis. The ratio of the use of IMF resources to total available quotas is higher during the third and fourth years after a quota review than during the first and second years after a review.

IMF officials are not shy about their desire to protect the budget. James Boughton, economic historian for the IMF explains, "The main challenge for the future is safeguarding the [IMF's] identity *and its resources*, so that it can continue to provide adequate support to its now universal membership."[5] IMF officials stress the importance of safeguarding Fund resources and providing loans. The IMF has certainly been known to make loans that were questionable. Indeed, balance of payments problems do not always precede IMF arrangements, even though this is mandated in the Articles of Agreement.

As another example, until recently, the IMF kept the details of IMF program conditions secret. This made it difficult to know if the IMF was enforcing conditions or simply engaging in lending to pad its budget. Today, IMF conditions are made public, but they are numerous and complicated, making it difficult to observe whether the IMF is enforcing what its arrangements require.

Yet, this does not imply that the organization is completely unaccountable. Economist Thomas Willett of Claremont McKenna College, agrees with Vaubel that, like any bureaucracy, the IMF has incentives to shirk some of its duties.[6] Yet, he recognizes that there is some accountability. The long chain of command may damage accountability, but it does not destroy it. The IMF is held accountable to an extent – but accountable to whom?

Sociologist Sarah Babb and economist Ariel Buira propose that the IMF is mainly accountable to the US. They agree with Vaubel that over time the procedures followed and the conditions imposed have become increasingly discretionary. While Vaubel views discretion as an indication that the IMF has achieved greater independence from its most powerful members, however, Babb and Buira argue that the change to discretionary rules "cannot be attributed primarily to internal bureaucratic factors, but rather responded to the demands of the Fund's most powerful organizational constituent: the US Treasury."[7] In their view, increasing reliance on discretionary rules came from pressure from the United States so that US favored nations would face weaker enforcement of conditionality than other countries.

The idea that the IMF is a tool of the US follows a "realist" view. "Realism" is an old and influential school of thought in the study of international relations, which views the power of international institutions with a great deal of skepticism. Realists believe that international institutions such as the IMF merely reflect the underlying interests of the powerful countries that created them. From this perspective, we should expect the IMF to follow the interests of its major shareholders – primarily the United States.

The influence of the United States

Protestors of the IMF, convinced the Fund is run by the US, are often surprised to learn that the United States only controls about 17.08 percent of the votes at the IMF. This may give the US veto power over certain important decisions that require an 85 percent majority, but it is a far cry from majority control of the Fund.

The IMF does not operate according to strict voting rules, however, as discussed in Chapter 1, the Managing Director, who usually chairs the Executive Board meetings, leads the IMF according to the "sense of the meeting." Thus, opposition to the US by smaller countries cannot be expressed through block voting, but must be voiced individually. The power of the US, not only at the IMF but in general, may discourage such opposition. Moreover, the Managing Director has been reported to rarely act against the will of the US since the US has veto power over his appointment and reappointment.[8]

Many scholars have therefore proposed that the US uses the IMF to pursue political objectives.[9] There are many anecdotes. For example, Zaire, a US Cold War ally, signed IMF arrangements in 1976, 1977, 1979, 1981, 1983, 1985, 1986, 1987, and 1989; while neighboring Angola, which leaned towards the Soviet Union, did not even join the IMF until 1989. Bessma Momani, a political scientist at Waterloo University, finds that the US pressured the IMF to grant lenient conditions to Egypt in 1987 and 1991 to help preserve the stability of the pro-Western Egyptian government during turbulent times.[10]

As a more recent example, it is suspected that the large IMF loan that Pakistan received in December 2001 was a payoff for the cooperation with the US invasion of Afghanistan (recall Box 1.7, Chapter 1). The size of the loan was indeed suspicious, as it was more than double the size of the previous loan agreement, which expired in September of that year. Yet, Pakistan was already on track to enter into a new IMF agreement in 2001, and given the country's long history of participation, it is difficult to prove that Pakistan would not have received a new IMF loan regardless of US influence. Momani makes a compelling case that although the US took credit for favorable treatment of Pakistan by the IMF, such treatment was likely to be forthcoming even if September 11 had never happened and the US did not seek Pakistan's assistance in its Afghanistan campaign.[11] Pakistan had participated in IMF arrangements in every year since 1993. Before that, the country had participated in IMF arrangements in 1958–1959, 1965–1966, 1968–1969, 1972–1975, 1977–1978, 1980–1983, and 1988–1991. As a Cold War ally of the US, it is possible that some of these arrangements were also politically driven, but this pattern of participation is typical of many developing countries. If Pakistan had decided *not* to help the US following September 11, however, would the IMF have treated the country harshly under pressure from Washington? This is an unobservable counterfactual.

Political motivations are difficult to prove – especially on a case by case basis. This is a central problem with anecdotal evidence – when dealing with only one observation at a time, it is difficult to sort out one explanation from another. Do economics, politics, or both explain Pakistan's IMF programs? What about other countries?

One way to address these questions is to look at a larger set of cases and perform comparisons. For example, Tony Killick, economist of the International Economic Development Group, reports that in about a third of 17 cases he studied, one of the more powerful members of the IMF intervened for political reasons to assure favorable treatment of the country.[12] Kendall Stiles, a political scientist at Brigham Young University, found that international politics influenced the IMF in six out of seven cases studied.[13] Even these larger studies, however, suffer from limitations. There is no measure of just how systematic is the pattern of international political influence. Also, these studies only look at countries that actually participate in IMF programs. What about countries that do not participate? Maybe the US pressures the IMF in other cases without effect. If so, then perhaps the IMF is not being used as a tool of foreign policy after all. Some comparisons with countries *not participating* in IMF programs are necessary.

Strom Thacker, a political scientist at Boston University, undertook the first systematic study of a large body of evidence on the question of US influence at the IMF. To test whether the US uses the IMF as a tool of foreign policy, he considered voting patterns at the United

Nations as a determinant of IMF programs. Thacker found that countries that voted along similar lines as the US were more likely to receive an IMF program than countries that did not. More specifically, countries that changed their voting patterns so that they became more similar to the US preferences were more likely to get an IMF conditioned loan, and countries that changed their voting against the US were less likely to get a loan. At first blush, it may seem strange to consider voting at the United Nations as meaningful – many votes are symbolic and most are not of great importance to the US. But Thacker was careful to include in his study only those votes that the US State Department had identified as "key votes." These were votes that the US had announced that it did care about.

By using statistical analysis of the experience of 87 countries (for a total of over 700 yearly observations), Thacker was able to control for other factors that determine IMF participation. He did find evidence that economic factors play an important role. The economic need for an IMF loan is a determinant of participation in an IMF program. But moving closer to the US in terms of voting on key issues at the United Nations also plays a significant role. A more recent study by Graham Bird and colleague Dane Rowlands of Carleton University confirms Thacker's point. In their 2001 study, they find voting proximity to the US to be a significant factor in IMF lending decisions, especially during the Cold War, although movement in voting patterns was not a significant factor in their study.[14]

Since Thacker's systematic study of US political influence over the IMF, others have explored other ways of measuring and testing US influence. For example, Randall Stone has looked at the connection between US foreign aid and IMF punishment for non-compliance with the conditions attached to IMF loans. Stone considers the amount of foreign aid that a country receives from the US to be a proxy for how important the country is to the US. He finds that countries receiving favorable amounts of US foreign aid are also likely to receive favorable treatment by the IMF.

Stone has undertaken two studies considering the effect of US foreign aid on IMF program punishment intervals, one on the post-communist countries of Eastern Europe, and one on Africa.[15] Both studies confirm his hypothesis: the more US foreign aid a country receives, the shorter the duration of punishment for IMF programs that fall into non-compliance. In addition to the statistical studies, Stone presents detailed case studies. For example, he shows that Russia, a country that was considered to be of great strategic importance to the US after the fall of Communism, received light punishments for non-compliance. In contrast, Poland, which was considered to be of much less importance to the US, faced a credible threat of punishment for noncompliance with its arrangements with the IMF.[16] Stone concludes, "although the United States holds a minority of votes, it does indeed call the shots at the IMF, as critics allege."[17]

In a series of recent studies, Axel Dreher, of the Swiss Federal Institute of Technology, Zurich, substantiates more evidence of international political influence over the IMF. In work with political scientist Nathan Jensen of Washington University, he finds that US allies receive IMF programs with fewer conditions attached.[18] In work with Jan-Egbert Sturm, also of the Swiss Federal Institute of Technology, Zurich, Dreher has found that IMF lending programs are used as bribes and rewards for countries that vote in the UN General Assembly not just with the US but with other powerful members of the Fund, including Japan, Germany, France and the United Kingdom.[19] In further work by Dreher, Sturm, and me, we find that countries serving as temporary members of the UN Security Council also receive favorable treatment from the IMF in terms of both program participation and number of conditions.[20] Our argument is that because the UN Security Council votes on issues important to the major shareholders of the IMF – issues such as imposing sanctions and going to war – UN Security Council members can count on favorable treatment from the Fund. Dreher's body of work with his colleagues contributes to the conclusion that the IMF is systematically used as a tool of foreign policy.

Voter influence over the IMF

The evidence that the IMF is influenced by international politics begs the question of how far back this control goes. Whose objectives does the US, for example, pursue through the IMF? Does the US use the IMF to further strategic interests or economic interests? Do the domestic politics of the US play a role? Do US voters actually have some degree of influence? A recent study by Lawrence Broz and Michael Hawes indicates that the answer to this last question might be yes.[21] Broz and Hawes consider the "microfoundations" of influence at the IMF: rather than consider the US as a single entity, they consider the preferences of the political actors within the US.

Specifically, Broz and Hawes analyze US Congressional votes on requests for quota increases in 1983 and 1998. Voting for a quota increase is a straightforward way to support the IMF – it increases the resources the Fund has for its lending activities. Which members of Congress voted in favor of such increases and which voted against? Broz and Hawes propose that US representatives in Congress responded to the preferences over the IMF of the voters in their districts and especially to the preferences of the contributors to their electoral campaigns.

Some members of Congress receive greater campaign contributions from "money-center" banks – banks that specialize in international banking such as Citibank, J. P. Morgan Chase, Bank of America, Citicorp, First Chicago, and Bankers Trust. These money-center banks have a strong interest in supporting the IMF, since IMF lending can go to countries indebted to them. The presence of a strong IMF mitigates the risks that these banks face when lending to developing countries. If the IMF can bail the countries out of an economic crisis, there is a better chance that the countries will not default on loans they owe to these banks. Thus, US representatives who rely on campaign contributions from money-center banks should be more likely to support US quota increases for the IMF than members who do not.

This is precisely what Broz and Hawes find in their statistical analysis of the roll call votes in 1983 and 1998. The representatives who received campaign contributions from institutions like Citibank were more likely to vote in favor of increased funding to the IMF. The representatives less beholden to such banks were less likely to vote for a larger IMF. In general, the greater the proportion of campaign contributions that come from money-centered banks, the more likely a representative was to vote in favor of increasing the US contribution to the IMF.

Furthermore, Broz and Hawes present evidence that US Congress representatives are also responsive to the preferences of voters in their districts. What are the voter preferences over the IMF? They may come from more general preferences over globalization, as voters view the IMF as a force for global economic integration. High-skilled workers in the US – those with higher levels of education and training – favor global economic integration because they seek to purchase imported goods from developing countries and do not compete for jobs with the low skilled workers from these countries. In contrast, low-skilled workers in the US, who must compete for wages and jobs with the low-skilled and low-paid workers in developing countries, see global economic integration as a threat. Broz and Hawes reason that the proportion of high-skilled versus low-skilled workers in a Congressional representative's district should influence how the representative votes on increasing the US quota at the IMF. Members of the US House of Representatives who represent more low-skilled workers should vote against the IMF, as the IMF supports policies of increased global integration, while those representing high-skilled workers should support the IMF. These hypotheses are supported by the evidence Broz and Hawes analyze. They consider two variables to capture the average skill level of workers in each district: the share of district population with at least four years of college, and the share of district workers in executive, administrative, managerial, professional, and professional specialty occupations. Both of these variables, which are proxies for the share of high-skilled workers in a district, have a positive effect on House members' support for the IMF.[22]

Thus, individual citizens, at least those in the US, do appear to have an impact on the operations at the IMF. They appear to influence Congress, and Congress in turn has been decisive in determining the size of the IMF budget. Indeed, in 1983 Congress voted to increase the US quota, while in 1998 Congress voted against it.

Yet, what about the day-to-day activities of the Fund? What about the hundreds of IMF programs that have been approved by the IMF Executive Board? Is there evidence of direct US influence besides Thacker's finding about voting records at the United Nations? Broz and Hawes, as well as political scientists Thomas Oatley and Jason Yackee of the University of North Carolina, present evidence indicating that there is. Oatley and Yackee show that the amount of US bank exposure in a developing country is a determinant of the size of the IMF loans the country received.[23] Broz and Hawes find that the total amount of US lending as a proportion of a developing country's GDP is a significant predictor of both whether or not a country receives a loan and the size of the IMF loan as well. They test to see if the bank exposure of other countries has a similar effect and find that it does not. Only US bank exposure is a significant predictor. Broz and Hawes take this as evidence of the influence of US banks operating through US political channels – through Congress and the President to the US Director on the IMF Executive Board.

The independent effect of international financiers

US banks influence the IMF via the US government. Do private financial institutions also have direct influence over the IMF? Political scientist Erica Gould of the University of Virginia argues that they do.[24] Gould observes that the size of an IMF loan is often not sufficient for a country in economic crisis to balance its payments. "Supplemental financing" from various sources is thus commonplace. In addition to providing a loan, the IMF negotiates with other sources of international finance – such as the governments of developed countries, multilateral lending organizations, and private lending institutions – to provide "supplemental" loans. These "supplemental financiers" are willing to assist the IMF in bailing out developing countries because the IMF promises to monitor and enforce the economic conditions to improve countries' balance of payments situations, which in turn facilitates their own financial transactions and makes loan repayment more likely. Supplemental financing is often vital for the success of an IMF program because without it, the IMF loan may not be sufficient to bail a country out of an economic crisis. Supplemental financiers are thus in a strong position to make demands on the Fund about the design of an IMF program. These financiers have an interest in specifying the precise policy conditions that are attached to an IMF loan.

What types of policy conditions do these international creditors prefer? Creditor states and multilateral organizations may lend for political reasons, Gould argues. Indeed, as was explained above, the US may use the IMF to reward its friends and punish its enemies. If an IMF program is to be a reward, creditor states may push the IMF to require less stringent conditions. These types of supplemental financiers push for weak conditionality.

Private financial institutions are different and have different preferences. They lend for profit, not for aid. Not only do these supplemental financiers seek stringent conditions, they push for what Gould calls *bank-friendly* conditions. Some IMF arrangements spell out the specific requirement that the program country must pay back a commercial bank creditor. Thus, by acting as a supplemental financier, private financial institutions can use the enforcement power of the IMF to ensure repayment of the loans they extend to a country. This repayment is made a condition of the IMF arrangement and future IMF loans thus depend on repayment of private financial institutions first.

Gould describes several examples of bank-friendly conditions, including that the program country must (1) "set aside certain fiscal revenues to match ... international loans with fiscal revenues," (2) use a percentage of the IMF loan "for debt-reduction payments or replenishment of reserves," and (3) "make debt-service payments, as agreed with commercial banks and/or official creditors."[25]

Gould tests the influence of supplemental financiers using carefully collected data on more than 200 conditioned IMF arrangements in 20 countries from 1952 to 1995. Her statistical analysis reveals that when supplemental financing comes from private financial institutions, bank-friendly conditions are more common. The amount of lending and grants the country received from the US, on the other hand, was negatively associated with bank-friendly conditions. So, bank-friendly conditions were more likely when countries used private financial assistance, but less likely when the country received financing from the US. Even after economic variables that predict IMF lending were included, the private bank finding remained.[26]

In addition to her statistical work, Gould also recounts some shocking anecdotes. For example, an SBA with Ghana in 1983 stipulated that the IMF loan to Ghana be deposited directly in a Bank of Ghana account held at the Bank of England, and that the Bank of England was to transfer the deposit directly to the Standard Chartered Bank to repay a short term loan it had made to Ghana. So the IMF loan never even reached Ghana, but rather went directly to repay a commercial bank.[27]

Gould has done the first extensive work that systematically covers the details of IMF agreements – something Chapter 5 addresses. Her work shows that the IMF is influenced not only by its members directly, but also indirectly by private lending institutions whose supplemental financing is often required for an IMF program to be successful.

Summary

Who controls the IMF? The evidence presented in this chapter demonstrates that no single mechanism of control accounts for all of the actions of the IMF.

To an extent, accountability problems leave some room for the IMF to behave independently. Such problems account in part for the growth of the IMF staff and for excessive lending to developing countries before reviews of the IMF budget. This explains why the IMF does not always lend to countries facing severe crises – sometimes lending simply justifies the IMF budget. But this is not the only non-economic crisis reason for IMF lending.

To an extent, the United States, as the economically most powerful member, is able to use the IMF as a tool of foreign policy, pushing the IMF to pursue its political goals instead of the mandated economic goals of mitigating balance of payments problems. As such, the IMF lends to countries favored by the US and is less likely to lend to countries not favored. The excellent work in this area still leaves some important open questions: How does the US use its influence? Does it push most often to reward countries that cooperate with the US, countries that are strategic allies, or countries with strong economic ties to the US? And what about the other members of the IMF? A burgeoning area of research considers the extent to which other powerful members of the Fund – Japan, Germany, France, and the United Kingdom – also exert political pressure on the IMF.

To an extent, private financial institutions exert direct influence on the IMF. When supplemental financing is required from them because a country's balance of payments problems are so severe that the IMF loan alone is not sufficient, private financial institutions may be put in a position to shape the IMF economic program. In these situations, private financial institutions are likely to insist that the IMF impose the condition that they be repaid before future IMF loans can be distributed to the country.

For those who long for an idyllic international institution, these accounts of the IMF may seem disappointing. But what about the naïve suggestion that the IMF acts according to its mandate as laid out in the Articles of Agreement? Members contribute resources to the Fund supposedly for the institution to act as an international lender during times of economic crisis. Perhaps this view is not so naïve after all. None of the studies discussed in this chapter disputes that the IMF enters into arrangements with countries facing economic crises. The statistically significant findings discussed in this chapter held *even when economic factors were controlled for*. But those economic factors themselves *were also statistically significant*. It would have been truly disappointing if the standard economic variables failed to predict IMF program participation. The conclusion would have been that the IMF completely disregards its mandate and simply acts according to the influence of international and bureaucratic politics.

But this is not the case. As the next chapter shows, the expected economic factors definitely do play a role in the activities of the IMF. They do not tell the entire story – political factors at the international level and at the domestic level in developing countries do play a role. Yet, one should not ignore the fact that to a great extent the IMF is a *technocracy*. It is staffed by economists who pursue the very tasks laid out in the Articles of Agreement.

3 Why do governments participate in IMF programs?

Some of the evidence presented in the previous chapter might lead one to believe that US foreign policy concerns completely dominate the question of who gets loans from the IMF. Yet, economic conditions were also found to be significant factors in determining which countries participate in IMF programs. To the extent that economic factors have systematic effects on the patterns of participation in IMF programs, the IMF acts according to its mandate laid out in the Articles of Agreement. A country's level of development, its balance of payments situation, its foreign reserve position, and its level of foreign debt all influence IMF lending decisions. Technocratic concerns determine much of what goes on at the IMF.

It is also important to realize that participation in an IMF program is a *joint* decision between the IMF and the recipient country. International politics tell only part of the story. For there to be an IMF program, both the IMF and a government must agree on the details of the arrangement. This chapter presents the decision of the government to enter into an IMF program. This decision depends on a government's need for an IMF loan and on the desirability of IMF conditions. The country's economic situation and political constraints faced by the government both play a role.

Recall from Chapter 1 that an IMF program does not just consist of a loan; strings are attached in the form of policy conditions. These policies can be severe. The IMF views balance of payments shortfalls as a problem of excess demand for imports. To address such a problem, consumption of imports must be curtailed. This can be done by reducing public expenditures and raising taxes (fiscal austerity), by raising interest rates and restricting credit creation (tight monetary policy), and sometimes by devaluing the national currency.

Why would a government ever agree to such conditions? The obvious answer is that the country desperately needs the IMF loan.

Yet, as the next chapter discusses, economic imperatives tell only part of the story of why governments participate in IMF programs. Sometimes governments actually want specific IMF policy conditions to be imposed on them. There are various political stories, such as a scapegoat story, where governments seek to blame the IMF for poor economic performance. There is also a signaling story, where the government seeks to use the IMF to tie its hands to send a credible signal of its commitment to economic reform to investors and creditors. The most theorized political story, however, and the one most supported by both anecdotal and systematic evidence is a "leverage" or "tipping the balance" story, where governments use the outside pressure of the IMF to push through unpopular policies that the government actually wants to implement. Before turning to these political stories of participation, however, this chapter begins by addressing the evidence of the economic story of participation in IMF programs.

The need for a loan story

The standard story for why governments enter into IMF arrangements is that they face some kind of shortfall in foreign reserves. In one basic scenario, for example, a country may simply be importing more than it exports. To pay for goods from abroad, importers must use "hard currency," like the dollar, the yen, the pound or the euro. So importers exchange local currency. Without balanced exports, eventually local banks may begin to run out of hard currency to provide. When this happens, it becomes difficult to purchase important imports. These imports may include inputs required for the economy to function – such as tractor parts for agricultural activities to continue, or manufacturing inputs, or petroleum. They may also include food stuffs necessary for the very sustenance of the population. For its survival, a government may seek out an IMF loan of foreign currency in order to maintain at least the most important imports.[1]

What precipitates a situation like this? In some cases, this is due to a bad economic shock. For example, the country may be reliant on exports of one primary product to generate foreign exchange, and for reasons that have nothing to do with the country's economic policies, the world price for that product may drop dramatically. The lower price may be so severe that the country cannot generate enough foreign exchange through its exports to maintain its imports. A large balance of payments deficit may ensue, along with a drop in the country's foreign reserves. The country's government may turn to the IMF to help get through this economic shock.

In other cases, the need for an IMF loan may be due to bad policies. For example, a government may engage in public spending that outpaces tax revenue. Unsustainable levels of expenditure may lead the government to borrow from international creditors. If the public expenditures do not generate economic growth and are wasteful, the government may find itself unable to pay the service on its foreign debt. As foreign reserves are depleted to make debt payments, the government may turn to the IMF for a loan of additional foreign exchange, lest the country go into default with its creditors.

As described in Chapter 1, the Articles of Agreement mandate that the IMF can engage in temporary lending to its members for the purpose of addressing balance of payments problems. Obviously, then, balance of payments problems should predict when governments enter into IMF programs. Surprisingly, this is not born out in all studies. While some studies have found that increasing the balance of payments deficit is a good predictor of countries participating in IMF programs,[2] many studies have not found that the balance of payments is a statistically significant predictor.[3] My research shows that while the overall size of the balance of payments deficit matters, certain key components of the balance of payments do not. The current account – which measures credits minus the debits of goods, services, income, and current transfers – is not a strong predictor of participation in IMF programs.

Rather than simply rely on summaries of these previous studies (references are in the notes to this chapter), consider looking directly at data. Figure 3.1 presents the average current account balance of countries before and after they participate in IMF programs. The data on IMF program participation come from various IMF Annual Reports and are available from my web page: http://pantheon.yale.edu/~jrv9. The current account data come from *World Development Indicators*, which is published annually by the World Bank.[4] The data cover the period 1970–2000 for 174 countries, although there are not an equal number of observations per country because of missing current account data and because some countries become independent or cease to exist at different times. In total, there are 3,541 "country-year" observations of current account balance as a percentage of gross domestic product (GDP).[5] The average balance of payments deficit for the current account as a percentage of GDP for all observations is 4.14.

Figure 3.1 shows no clear-cut relationship between IMF participation and the current account – there is no obvious trend before or after participation. There is a peak average deficit of 6.46 percent of GDP the year before governments enter into IMF programs, but there are also peaks of 6.23 percent of GDP five years before participation and

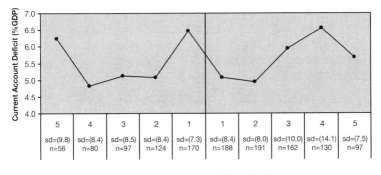

Figure 3.1 Average current account deficit before and during IMF program participation: *no clear pattern emerges.*

6.55 percent of GDP four years after participation begins. The average current account deficit appears to drop the first and second years after participation begins, but it is also relatively low two to four years before participation begins. Figure 3.1 also reports relatively wide standard deviations for each average current account deficit, which indicate a wide variety of experiences before and after countries begin participating in IMF programs.

As this chapter shows below, using more sophisticated statistical tests, there appears to be a weak correlation between the current account and participation in IMF programs in the expected direction – governments are more likely to participate when the current account deficit is high – but the relationship is not statistically significant.

Instead of looking at the current account balance, what about simply looking at a country's stock of foreign reserves? Note that the Articles of Agreement also indicate that the IMF should lend to countries facing shortfalls in foreign reserves. Existing studies confirm that this variable does predict participation in IMF programs.[6] Again, rather than rely on other studies, consider the data presented in Figure 3.2. This figure presents average foreign reserves – measured as a proportion of the country's average monthly imports – before and during IMF program participation. The foreign reserves data come from *World Development Indicators*. From 1965 to 1998 there are 3,266 country-year observations for 168 independent countries. The average level of foreign exchange held on reserve is equal to 3.3 times the monthly imports. When countries are observed participating in IMF programs, reserves average just 2.7 times monthly imports. When countries are observed not participating,

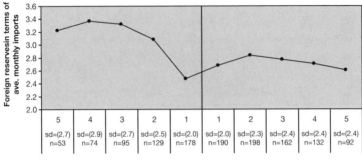

Figure 3.2 Average foreign reserves before and during IMF program
participation: *low foreign reserves predicts turning to the IMF.*

reserves average 3.6 times monthly imports. Simply stated, reserves are
lower for program countries. Figure 3.2 reveals that there is a pattern
driving this. Foreign reserves[7] plummet the year before countries enter
into IMF programs. They appear to rebound slightly, perhaps because of
the loans associated with IMF programs, but remain low while countries
participate. More rigorous analysis of these data – presented later in
the chapter – indicates that this relationship is statistically significant.

Governments may also need to turn to the IMF for a loan when the
service on their outstanding debt becomes too burdensome. Several
statistical studies show that high levels of indebtedness are associated
with IMF program participation.[8] A look at the data also confirms
this finding from the literature. From 1970 to 2000, there are 3,063
observations of debt service from 134 countries. The debt service data,
measured as a percentage of gross national income (GNI), come from
World Development Indicators. Overall, the average debt service is 5.07
percent of GNI. For countries participating in IMF programs, average
debt service is 6.40 percent of GNI, but when countries are not participating, the average is 4.03 percent of GNI. Figure 3.3 shows that on
average, debt service increases one to two years before countries turn
to the IMF. There is a sharp increase the first year a country turns to
the IMF, and as participation continues debt service drops slightly –
perhaps because of successful debt renegotiations – but remains higher
than in countries not participating in IMF programs. Again more
rigorous analyses – presented below – confirm that this pattern is
statistically significant as well.

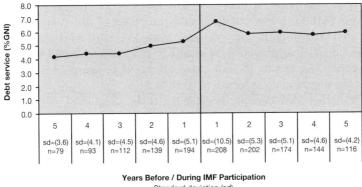

Figure 3.3 Average debt service before and during IMF program participation: *high debt service predicts turning to the IMF.*

Recidivism and sovereignty

Economic factors do explain – in part – participation in IMF programs. But they do not tell the whole story. One non-economic factor that has been cited in the literature to predict IMF program participation is past participation.[9] According to Graham Bird, the reason for this lies in the lack of IMF programs producing sustainable economic growth: "… as long as Fund-backed programs fail to effectively encourage economic growth as a top priority, many developing countries will remain Fund recidivists… ."[10] Indeed, the most obvious explanation for this finding is that countries turning to the IMF for economic reasons in the past are likely to have economic problems again and, thus, enter another IMF arrangement.

Yet, past participation is such a strong predictor of present participation that this factor is statistically significant even after one controls for economic factors. To understand what this means, imagine that two countries face the exact same economic circumstances but one of them has participated in IMF programs in the past and the other has never participated before. The country with the past experience is substantially more likely to enter into a new IMF arrangement than the other country. This implies that past participation in IMF programs makes a country more likely to return to the IMF, regardless of the economic impacts of IMF programs.

As Figure 3.4 shows, the proportion of countries entering into IMF programs with and without past experience has remained fairly steady over time. The figure includes all observations of countries not participating in IMF programs and depicts the percentage of them that entered into an IMF program the following year. The pattern is clear: the proportion of countries entering into IMF programs for countries with past experience is two to four times greater than the proportion of countries that have no experience.

Recall that IMF lending is intended to be temporary. Chapter 1 described different lending facilities at the IMF in terms of differing time horizons. SBAs are intended to last between one to two years, while EFF, SAF, and ESAF/PRGF programs are intended to last three to four years. Yet, the typical pattern is for a country to sign consecutive agreements. Part of this can be explained by a crisis situation not allowing enough time to plan a full four year program. When a country is facing a severe crisis, the IMF may quickly put together an SBA that lasts one year, and then begin a four year PRGF. But this can only explain some cases. It cannot explain the overall pattern of extensive participation among developing countries.

Consider the following data: since the first IMF agreement in 1952 until 2000, governments entered into 936 separate IMF arrangements (SBA, EFF, SAF, and ESAF/PRGF) that spanned a total of 1,838 country-years. Some of these arrangements lasted only one year, others dragged on for over five years (for example, Honduras entered into an ESAF program on 24 July 1992 that lasted until 24 July 1997). The average length of a spell of participation – where a spell is defined as

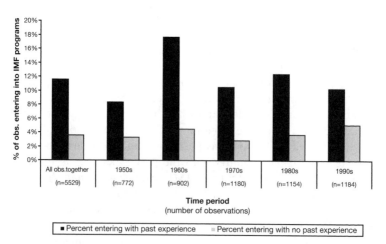

Figure 3.4 Entering into IMF programs: *with past participation versus without past participation.*

consecutive years of participation in conditioned IMF arrangements, regardless of how many times agreements were resigned – was 5.5 years.[11]

In the meantime, countries with a past history of IMF participation were likely to *return* again to the IMF. For countries with a past history of IMF programs, the average spell of non-participation was 6.4 years. On the one hand, this figure includes spells of non-participation that may continue beyond the year 2000, so it may underestimate how long countries can go without the IMF. On the other hand, it also includes spells of non-participation for the developed world, where countries used the IMF early on and have never returned. For example, the United States entered into SBAs on July 22 in 1963 and 1964, and Japan entered into an SBA on January 19, 1962 and March 11, 1964 – neither country ever returned. Excluding countries with per capita incomes greater than $10,000,[12] the average spell of non-participation was just 5.2 years. So the overall typical experience of developing countries is to spend about five years participating in IMF programs, followed by about five years not participating, followed by five more years of participation, et cetera. And then there are the extreme cases. Table 3.1 presents the countries that had consecutive years of IMF participation for ten years or more.

What explains this so-called recidivism? Certainly part of the reason that countries return to the Fund again and again is that IMF programs have been largely unsuccessful in promoting economic development, as Chapter 4 describes. Indeed, to the extent that IMF policies hurt economic growth, they may set the stage for continued reliance on IMF loans. In this sense, IMF programs have been compared to an addictive and harmful drug.[13] If recidivism were driven entirely by poor economic performance, however, then the correlation between past participation and continued participation would disappear once one accounted for economic factors. It does not. Indeed, statistical work that distinguishes between the probability of entering into IMF programs from the probability of continuing IMF programs reveals that economic factors predict entering far better than they predict continuing. There seems to be something about past participation that actually causes countries to return and continue participation.

One possibility is that participation in IMF programs establishes connections between individuals in a country's government and individuals at the IMF. Such interpersonal connections may lower the transaction and negotiation costs of future agreements, thus making the next IMF program more readily available. There have been no empirical studies of such a possibility, although there is evidence that individual connections matter. Economists Robert Barro of Harvard

Table 3.1 Countries with extensive continuous participation in IMF programs

10 year spells	13 year spells	18 year spells
Honduras (1966)	Paraguay (1969)	Peru (1971)
Haiti (1967)	Korea, South (Rep.) (1977)	Colombia (1974)
Chile (1970)	Uruguay (1987)	Costa Rica (1997)
Gambia (1991)	Sierra Leone (1989)	Argentina (2000)
Ghana (1992)	Madagascar (1992)	Philippines (2000)
Ecuador (1992)		
Lesotho (1997)	*14 year spells*	*19 year spells*
Burkina Faso (2000)	Senegal (1992)	Mali (2000)
Nicaragua (2000)	Morocco (1993)	
Mongolia (2000)	Mauritania (1998)	*20 year spells*
Bulgaria (2000)	Gabon (1999)	Panama (1987)
Romania (2000)	Mozambique (2000)	Jamaica (1996)
	Uganda (2000)	Togo (1998)
11 year spells		
Turkey (1971)	*15 year spells*	*21 year spell*
Philippines (1981)	Bolivia (1970)	Haiti (1990)
Somalia (1990)	Liberia (1977)	
Mexico (1993)	Zaire (1990)	
Jordan (1999)	Guinea (2000)	
El Salvador (2000)	Bolivia (2000)	
Guyana (2000)		
	16 year spells	
12 year spells	El Salvador (1973)	
Kenya (1986)	Yugoslavia (1986)	
Zambia (1987)		
Cote d'Ivoire (1992)	*17 year spells*	
Malawi (1999)	Guyana (1983)	
Benin (2000)		

Note: Year indicates when the spell ended. If 2000, the spell may have continued.

University and Jong-Wha Lee of Korea University study the relationship between the proportion of IMF staff who come from a particular
country and the likelihood of that country participating in an IMF
program. They find that, in fact, countries with more nationals on the
staff of the IMF are more likely to participate.[14]

Yet another way of thinking about the recidivist phenomenon is to
ask the reverse question: Why are countries with *no* past experience
less likely to enter into an IMF program in the first place? The answer
may have to do with national sovereignty. In particular, it has to do with
the domestic audience costs of participating in IMF programs – the

"sovereignty costs" of participation. When a government enters into an IMF program, opposition to the government can accuse it of "selling out" to the international institution.[15] As the IMF has come to symbolize Neo-Western Imperialism in the minds of many throughout the developing world, this can be a serious accusation, one that has led to protests and evening rioting in the streets against governments. Never having submitted to the IMF can be a source of national pride. The first government in a country's history to submit to IMF conditionality often faces a severe cost for sacrificing sovereignty.

In a country where IMF programs have become business as usual, however, the costs of "selling out" are smaller. The IMF may not be popular, but it is difficult for opposition to claim that the current leadership is selling out by signing an IMF arrangement if many previous leaders have also done so. Indeed, if the opposition leaders have ever been in power, it is likely that they themselves have actually signed IMF arrangements. The argument is thus that past participation in IMF programs lowers domestic sovereignty costs of participation and makes governments more likely to return to the IMF again in the future. If a government can point to other examples of leaders in a country's history who turned to the IMF, the stigma of bowing to the IMF is lower.

The sovereignty cost story can help explain a peculiar regional pattern of participation: IMF programs were prevalent throughout Latin America during the 1960s and 1970s, but many developing African countries did not participate until the 1980s. The explanation goes as follows:

In the early years of IMF programs, there was no stigma associated with participation. The institution had been intended to help mainly Western European countries, and the first arrangements were with them. Along with the European countries, developing countries in Latin America entered into SBAs. *By 1965, all Latin American countries had participated in an IMF SBA.* During this time period it was difficult to see IMF participation as a sacrifice of national sovereignty – even the Western superpower, the United States, completed a stint of participation in 1963/4, signing two consecutive arrangements. The sovereignty costs in terms of "selling out" to the powers of Western capitalism were low, if a factor at all.

As the rigors of conditionality increased and the IMF became exclusively focused on just developing countries, sovereignty costs increased. By the time conditionality and the "sell out" stigma had become severe, Latin American countries already had years of experience with the IMF. This is not to say that people opposed to IMF did not accuse their governments of selling out when they signed IMF arrangements – they certainly did – but the costs of such accusations were lower in countries with longer histories of IMF programs.

Countries with little to no history of IMF programs by the late 1970s, on the other hand, faced high sovereignty costs of being the first government in a country's history to submit to the IMF. Such was the case for many African countries. In the early 1960s, when sovereignty costs were still low, most African countries were only just gaining independence. These countries were simply not around to enter into IMF programs when sovereignty costs were at their lowest. Since the IMF stigma had grown by the time these countries were in need of IMF financial assistance, many African countries resisted signing a conditioned IMF arrangement. They sought loans and grants from other sources and from IMF unconditioned facilities.

A good example of this phenomenon is the case of Nigeria. No government of Nigeria ever signed an IMF arrangement until 1987, even though the country faced a severe economic need for an IMF loan throughout the 1980s. Indeed, Nigerian governments first started negotiating with the IMF for a program in 1981. From 1981 to 1987, three different leaders were in power. All of them considered an IMF program – even entering into negotiations with the Fund – but all of them decided against an IMF arrangement. The sticking point was not austerity policy. Each leader during this period – democratically elected President Alhaji Shehu Shagari (1979–1983), and dictators Major General Muhammadu Buhari (1984–1985) and Major General Ibrahim Babangida (1985–1993) – pushed through high levels of economic austerity. The sticking point during the IMF negotiations was the devaluation of the national currency, the naira, which was considered by many to be a symbol of national sovereignty. Shagari announced that Nigeria would "not be dictated to" by the IMF.[16] Buhari proved his independence by pushing through economic austerity so severe it went *beyond* what many advised – all the while he refused IMF assistance. Babangida eventually signed an IMF program in 1987, but it was not until he had pushed through all of the conditions the IMF would demand on his own – before actually signing. He made known to the Nigerian public that all IMF policy conditions had been already met, so that the IMF arrangement involved just the loan.

When Babangida had first come into power in 1985, he had tested the water. In order to gauge just how strongly public sentiment opposed the IMF, Babangida invited the entire country to participate in what he called a "town meeting" on the IMF. People responded. The *New York*

Times reported that "Day after day on dusty street corners, in tiny shops and air conditioned offices, people are arguing, waving fists and shouting about the International Monetary Fund."[17] As protest raged in the streets, Babangida warned people to expect sacrifices whether an agreement was signed or not. Yet, he promised that "whatever decision we take, whether for or against [an IMF arrangement], I maintain that it is going to be decision based on what the Nigerian populace wants."[18]

People were opposed to the IMF. Protest came from all sectors of society: labor, business, university professors, students, and traditional leaders. Headlines such as "IMF Loan: A Tentacle of Capitalism" and "IMF: What For?" appeared in Nigerian newspapers. Nigerians preferred to tighten their belts without IMF assistance than to give up their national sovereignty. To widespread support, Babangida eventually suspended all IMF negotiations and declared a tough austerity program by which Nigeria would go it alone. The new austerity measures included reducing petroleum subsidies (doubling gasoline prices), public divestment from agriculture production, hotels, food and beverage industries and electrical manufacturing, and new taxes on corporate profits, dividends and rents.[19] Babangida imposed economic austerity, as if under an IMF program, but without an IMF loan. When world petroleum prices dropped again in 1986, the government devalued the naira. At this point, the IMF publicly announced that it was willing to grant Nigeria a loan, since the government had complied with all IMF economic policy conditions *ex ante*.[20]

With the stain of submitting to IMF policy conditions gone, Nigeria finally entered into its first SBA in January 1987. The country had held off the IMF for over five years of economic crisis with its own economic austerity before accepting an IMF loan with policy conditions attached. Yet after signing its first IMF arrangement, Nigeria entered into its second IMF arrangement in February 1989, and its third arrangement in January 1991. Once the ice was broken, the country was more likely to sign again and again.

One reason, therefore, that countries with no previous experience with IMF programs are less likely to enter into an IMF arrangement even when facing bad economic conditions is that governments face a more severe stigma for sacrificing national sovereignty in these situations.

One region of the world, however, does not fit this sovereignty cost story: Eastern Europe. Many Eastern European governments happily embraced IMF economic reform programs after the fall of Communism in the early 1990s. With the ideological shift towards the West, bringing in the IMF did not have a negative anti-Western stigma.

Rather, many governments argued that IMF policies, while costly in the short run, were needed for prosperity in the long run. Not everyone agreed that the governments advocated the correct policies, but since the governments were forthrightly in agreement with the IMF, they were not accused of "selling out." Instead, some governments used the weight of the IMF to help push through unpopular policies.

Bringing in the IMF to gain leverage over opposition is a tactic that has been used elsewhere as well. Before he was deposed from power, Shagari administration officials in Nigeria admitted (under the condition of anonymity) that "the whole idea of bringing in the IMF is to get the alibis to persuade the politicians of what we need to do."[21] While sovereignty costs proved too high for Shagari to actually enter into an IMF program, the need for an IMF loan was not the only reason his administration first opened negotiations with the IMF for a program. The government was also seeking international leverage to push through the unpopular austerity measures preferred by the government. This leads to a domestic political story of why governments enter into IMF programs.

The domestic desire for conditions

Sometimes the key to understanding IMF participation is as much political as economic. There are three political stories of why governments may want conditions imposed: a *blame* story, a *signaling* story, and a *leverage* story.

The most obvious is the *blame* story. Governments may desire conditionality so they can blame the IMF for unpopular policies. Political scientist Karen Remmer of Duke University contends that the presence of the IMF "allows authorities to attempt to shift blame for austerity to the Fund" and that the "power of the IMF remains a useful myth to explain difficult economic decisions."[22] Economists Sebastian Edwards of the University of California at Los Angeles and Julio Santaella of the Instituto Tecnológico Autónomo de México argue that governments facing domestic opposition to devaluation get the IMF to do their "dirty work": "By involving multinational bodies in the decision-making process, local politicians can shield themselves from the political fallout associated with unpopular policies."[23] Generally, Vaubel states that international organizations enable politicians "to shirk domestic responsibility for unpopular policies."[24]

To test this story, political scientist Alastair Smith of New York University and I looked at the effect of IMF programs on the survival rates of leaders. If the IMF is an effective scapegoat, participating in an IMF program should increase survival rates after economic circumstances are accounted for.[25] We found, however, that being under an IMF program only increases survival rates under certain conditions. Among democracies, we found that IMF programs had the effect of increasing survival rates only among leaders who *inherited* IMF programs. Democratically elected leaders can effectively blame the IMF for economic problems if the previous administration originally entered the IMF arrangement. The reason for this is that a government that enters into an IMF arrangement and blames the IMF for bad policy advice appears impotent. The IMF may be used as a scapegoat, but not by the government that originally brought in the IMF.

A second political story is *signaling*. One reason governments argue that the program is necessary, even if the policies themselves are painful, is that the IMF program sends a "signal" to investors and creditors that the country is a good risk. The pain of economic austerity indicates that the country is willing to pay a high price to keep its promises of repaying debt and that the country is dedicated to maintaining a safe environment for investors. The IMF "seal of approval" is supposed to bring in what has become known as "catalytic finance."

Evidence in favor of a "seal of approval" effect, however, is weak. Economists Graham Bird and Dane Rowlands have found no evidence that investment increases when countries participate in IMF programs.[26] Nathan Jensen has found that participation in IMF programs actually has a negative effect on foreign direct investment in developing countries.[27] There is one piece of evidence, however, supporting the signaling story. Political scientists Nancy Brune of Yale University, Geoffrey Garrett of University of Southern California, and Bruce Kogut of INSEAD find that the value of national assets that are privatized under the auspices of an IMF program are significantly higher than the value of assets privatized without the IMF.[28] They argue that this is because privatizing under the IMF sends a signal to potential investors that the privatization process is credible. Perhaps the most powerful signal IMF programs can send, however, is a negative one for countries whose programs fall apart. Rejecting the IMF is costly because it limits access to IMF credit[29] and sends negative signals to creditors[30] and investors.[31] The country as a whole may suffer from such negative signals.

The high costs of rejecting the IMF once under an IMF program are the key to the *leverage* story of IMF participation. As Stanley Fischer, the former First Deputy Managing Director of the IMF explains, "Policy conditionality can be interpreted as a ... penalty, as seen from the viewpoint of the borrower country's policy makers."[32]

Yet, many have argued that a reform-oriented executive may want the IMF to impose conditions to help push through unpopular policies. Political scientist Robert Putnam of Harvard University cites IMF negotiations with Italy in 1974 and 1977 as instances where "domestic conservative forces exploited the IMF pressure to facilitate policy moves that were otherwise infeasible internally."[33] He follows the work of economist Luigi Spaventa of the University of Rome, who argues that even "the unions and the Communists actually favored the austerity measures, but found the IMF demands helpful in dealing with their own internal [domestic] constituents."[34] James Bjork makes a similar observation about Poland. He contends "that most of the macroeconomic program imputed to IMF conditionality can be more accurately traced to economic imperatives or to domestic Polish political factors."[35] Economist Avinash Dixit of Princeton University claims that when "domestic constituents press for protection, subsidies, or inflationary finance, the treasuries can point to the conditions imposed by [the IMF] in return for much needed project loans or foreign currency."[36] This line of argumentation follows a broader political phenomenon described by a prominent political scientist of the twentieth century, Thomas Schelling: "The power to constrain an adversary may depend on the power to bind oneself."[37] Here, the power to bind oneself comes from the IMF.

How exactly does an IMF agreement help to push through unpopular reforms? Economist Allan Drazen of the University of Maryland suggests one mechanism. Suppose an executive wishes to change a government policy, such as expenditures on defense, but faces opposition. Say the opposition has veto power over policy change in this area. A lucrative IMF loan can help the executive persuade this "veto player" to approve the policy change, lest they forgo the next installment of the IMF loan.[38] Failing to comply with IMF programs also has costs in addition to not receiving the loan installment, since creditors and investors follow signals from the IMF.

One key to the leverage story is that executives enter into IMF arrangements without any formal domestic ratification process. Recall from Chapter 1 that IMF arrangements are explicitly not legal international agreements. Instead, IMF arrangements are spelled out in a "Letter of Intent," written by IMF staff and government officials and formally sent from the country's executive branch – recognized as the country's "proper authority" over the economy – to the IMF Managing Director. The Managing Director subsequently brings it before the IMF Executive Board for approval. Once the Board approves the Letter of Intent, the country is under an IMF program.

The approval of potential opponents to IMF policies who are in a position to block policy change – such as the legislature in a presidential system or a coalition partner in a parliamentary system – is not required for the executive to enter into an IMF arrangement. The approval of these "veto players" is bypassed, and the payoffs for enacting policy change have been altered. Now, the potential veto players must oppose not just the finance ministry but also the IMF. Failure to enact policy change becomes more costly because the IMF may restrict access to loans, it may preclude debt rescheduling with creditors who require an IMF arrangement to be in good standing, and it may result in decreased investment if investors take cues from the IMF.[39] These increased costs may lead veto players to approve of policy changes that they otherwise would have opposed.

Such a strategy is available to executives in different types of regimes – democracies and dictatorships alike. Political scientist Louis Pauly of the University of Toronto tells the story of a finance minister of a developing country who "specifically requested the managing director of the IMF to include in the routine surveillance report on his country a reference to the need to cut military expenditures … [T]he ruse apparently achieved its objective of adding weight to the views of the minister."[40] In another dictatorship, the reform-oriented government of President Ali Hassan Mwinyi used an IMF agreement in 1986 to put pressure on socialist leadership in the Chama Cha Mapinduzi revolutionary party that dominated Tanzanian politics to increase interest rates and cut public spending.[41]

Under democracy in Brazil, where President Cardoso entered into an IMF arrangement at the end of 1998, the Fund called for Brazil to meet certain conditions in return for a loan: cutting overall federal expenditures by 20 percent, cutting federal infrastructure projects by 40 percent, and reforming the social security system.[42] President Cardoso had been trying for years to get the approval for some of these measures but met resistance from within his governing coalition. After the East Asian financial crisis, Cardoso presented the changes as necessary to win IMF approval: "The whole world is watching us, watching to see if we'll be able to resolve the crisis."[43] Under such scrutiny, those resisting reform acquiesced on some issues, and the pace of reforms stepped up.[44]

As another example, consider Uruguay, where the executive entered into an IMF arrangement in 1990 despite a strong reserve position and despite surpluses in both the current account and the overall balance of payments. Uruguay did not need an IMF loan, but the newly elected president, Luis Alberto Lacalle, faced tough opposition to his unpopular program of economic reform. Over the course of his administration, his coalition party and eventually even his own party abandoned him. Lacalle had few domestic allies for his reform program, and so he brought in the IMF to have conditions imposed. While he was unable to push through his entire program, he had many successes, notably recording the highest budget surplus in Uruguay's history. Although a majority of legislators (even many from his own party) denounced Lacalle, the legislature reluctantly voted in favor of measures demanded by the IMF.[45]

One can go on and on with anecdotes, but are there more systematic ways to test this story? One possibility is to consider measures of resistance to policy change that vary across countries and over time.

IMF programs can most help to change policy when there is greater resistance to policy change. Political scientist George Tsebelis of UCLA argues that systematic resistance to policy change is in part a function of the number of veto players in a political system.[46] The intuition behind his argument is straightforward: policy change is less likely when more people are required to agree.[47] The number of actors who must agree – the number of veto players – depends on the political system. In most dictatorships, there is one just actor – either a single dictator, or a single party. In presidential systems, the president and the legislature must agree. In multi-party parliamentary systems, the governing coalition may include various political parties who must agree.[48] As the number of veto players increases, the probability that one of the veto players is opposed to policy change also increases.[49] In such a situation, the outside pressure of an IMF arrangement may be useful to force through a change in policy.

Figure 3.5 shows the rates of participation in IMF programs for different numbers of veto players.[50] The figure presents 1,296 country-year observations of 128 developing countries (per capita income less than $8,000 1995 PPP[51]) from 1975 to 2000, where the average number of veto players is 2 and the median number of veto players is 1. Note that the figure depicts the proportion of governments entering into IMF programs – i.e. governments that are already participating are not considered.

The figure shows a clear upward trend in the rates at which governments enter into IMF arrangements, although the trend is attenuated when there are too many veto players in the political system.[52] This may be due in part to the fact that countries with many veto players tend to be more economically developed, and such countries tend not to turn to the IMF for a loan. This possibility illustrates the importance of holding constant – or "controlling" for – economic factors

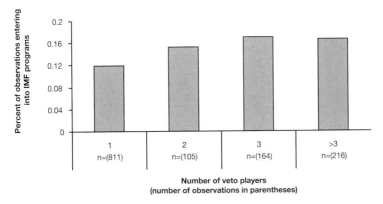

Figure 3.5 IMF participation by number of veto players.

Note: Per capita income < $8000.

when testing this story. Besides controlling for per capita income, it is important to hold constant other economic variables that have been addressed. This is especially important because it is possible that countries with many veto players are simply more likely to have economic crises. The additional veto players may make these political systems less able to make economic policy adjustments, so governments end up needing an IMF loan for economic reasons. To check for this, consider a more rigorous statistical test, which can account for these other determinants of IMF participation.

Estimating the probability of entering IMF programs statistically

Throughout this chapter, references have been made to "more rigorous statistical tests." This section presents such a test.[53] Some of the discussion is technical but intuitions are also provided. The purpose of this section is to test for the relationship between the number of veto players in a political system and IMF participation, as well as test for the effects of the other variables discussed in this chapter: per capita income, current account balance, foreign reserves, debt service, and past participation. This section reinforces what has already been covered in the chapter for readers curious about what a more rigorous statistical test would look like. For readers content with the basic summary provided above, this section can be skipped.

What kind of statistical model should one employ when testing stories of IMF participation? Note that the argument about the effects of veto players in a political system is not about participation in general, but rather about the likelihood of *entering* into IMF programs. Thus, the statistical model used here is called "dynamic" because it accounts for a transition over time – *entering* into IMF programs. (As discussed in the section above on "recidivism," the continuation of IMF programs is a different story.) The easiest way to understand the dynamic model is to imagine all of the observations of countries *not participating* in an IMF program, then ask: Which of them, *the following year*, enter into an IMF arrangement, and under what circumstances with respect to the "variables" per capita income, current account, foreign reserves, debt service, past participation, and number of veto players? The statistical model (called "dynamic logit") estimates the likelihood of entering into an IMF program based on the observed values of the "variables" included in the model. There are two basic questions the statistical model allows one to address: (1) what is the direction of the relationship between each "variable" and the likelihood of entering into IMF arrangements, and (2) how strong is the relationship – is it due just to luck or is it a systematic relationship that holds with some degree of regularity?

In Table 3.2 below, the column labeled "coefficient" reports the direction and magnitude of the relationship, and the column labeled "*p*-value" reports the probability that the relationship is due to just luck – a high score indicates that the relationship does not hold for many cases, while a low score in this column indicates a high chance of a systematic relationship.

The results presented in Table 3.2 confirm and summarize all of the results that were reported in this chapter. Let us go through the coefficients one by one. First, there is the "constant" term, which is like a variable that is coded 1 for all observations. The coefficient on the constant is estimated simply as part of the baseline probability. Otherwise, it really has no other substantive interpretation worth discussing

Table 3.2 Estimating the probability of entering into a spell of IMF arrangements using dynamic logit

Variable	Coefficient	p-value
Constant	− 1.81	0.00
Per capita income ($1,000s)	− 0.27	0.00
Current account (% GDP)	0.01	0.54
Foreign reserves (in months of imports)	− 0.17	0.00
Debt service (% exports)	0.02	0.00
Past participation	0.88	0.00
log(# of veto players)	0.40	0.02
Number of observations	684	

Box 3.1 **Dynamic logit**

For readers looking for a more technical interpretation of Table 3.2, the coefficient times the value of the variable is equal to the natural logarithm of the odds ratio of entering an IMF program:

$$\text{coefficient} \times \text{variable} = \ln\left[\frac{\Pr(entering)}{\Pr(not\ entering)}\right]$$

So a positive significant coefficient indicates that the variable increases the probability of entering into IMF agreements; a negative coefficient indicates that the variable decreases the probability of entering into IMF agreements.

As for interpreting whether the relationship is systematic or just a weak correlation driven by luck, the "*p*-value" for each coefficient indicates the probability that the true relationship between the variable and the likelihood of entering into IMF programs is zero. In other words, it is the probability that we *cannot* safely reject the null hypothesis that there is no relationship. Only if the *p*-value is low can one have confidence that there is a systematic relationship between the variable and the probability of participation. In the social sciences, we typically look for a *p*-value of less than 0.05.

here. It is, however, worth noting the estimated baseline probability of entering into IMF programs. This will help understand the impact of the other variables below. Holding all variables in the specification to their median values, the estimated baseline probability of entering into a spell of IMF arrangements is 0.15. Considering that the proportion of actually observed transitions into IMF programs is 0.14 in this sample, this is a fairly close baseline probability.

Per capita income (measured in $1,000s 1985 PPP) has a negative effect: –0.27. This effect is statistically significant: note the extremely low *p*-value of 0.00. Quite systematically, countries with higher per capita incomes are less likely to enter into IMF programs. To give this result more substance, suppose there are two identical "median" countries which have the same current account balance, level of foreign reserves, debt service, past participation and number of veto players – all at the median values for these variables. Yet, they differ in one respect. One has a per capita income that equals the median – $2, 251 – and the other has a higher per capita income, say, $4,382 (one standard deviation above the median). The country with the lower per capita income has a 0.15 probability of entering into an IMF program, while the country with the higher per capita income has only a 0.09 probability of entering into an IMF program. This is a substantial difference, cutting the likelihood of entering an IMF arrangement by one third. The implication is clear: more economic development, less reliance on IMF loans.

The effect of current account – with a coefficient of 0.01 – is not statistically significant. Note the high p-value of 0.54. This is consistent with the discussion above and the presentation of data in Figure 3.1. Current account balance does not predict entering into IMF programs.

The –0.17 effect of foreign reserves, however, is statistically significant (p-value of 0.00). When countries have higher foreign reserves, measured in terms of average monthly imports, they are less likely to enter into IMF programs. Substantively, if foreign reserves were to increase from the median value of 2.85 times monthly imports by one standard deviation up to 6.21 times monthly imports, the probability of entering into an IMF program would go from the baseline probability of 0.15 down to 0.09. The effect is of a similar magnitude to the effect of economic development. Countries are more likely to turn to the IMF when they face a shortfall in foreign reserves.[54]

Debt service has a positive and significant effect of 0.02 (p-value of 0.00). When debt service (measured as a percentage of exports of goods and services) goes up, a country is more likely to turn to the IMF. If debt service were to increase from its median value of 13.4 percent of exports by one standard deviation to 14.4 percent of exports, the probability of entering into an IMF program would go from 0.15 up to 0.19.

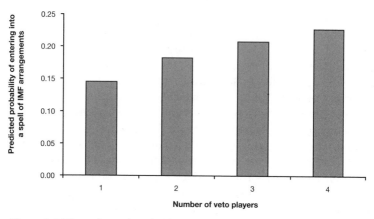

Figure 3.6 The estimated probability of entering into IMF arrangements by number of veto players (holding other variables constant).

Table 3.3 Estimating the probability of entering into a spell of IMF arrangements using dynamic logit with the larger sample

Variable	Coefficient	p-value
Constant	− 2.13	0.00
Per capita income ($1,000s)	− 0.31	0.00
Past participation	1.08	0.00
log(# of veto players)	0.30	0.03
Number of observations	2,140	

Past participation also predicts returning to the IMF. The positive coefficient of 0.88 is highly significant (*p*-value of 0.00). As noted above, the baseline probability of entering into a spell of IMF programs is 0.15. This is for countries that have already experienced IMF program participation in their past (the median country has already participated). For countries that have never participated, however, the probability of entering is a mere 0.07. This is a powerful effect. Imagine two identical countries that have the sample median level for the control variables – per capita income, current account, foreign reserves, debt service, and number of veto players – but one has already participated in IMF programs and the other never has. The one with past participation is more than *twice* as likely to participate as the one that never has! This can either be interpreted as recidivism or as evidence of the importance of sovereignty costs for first-time countries. This is consistent with what was presented about Nigeria above. There was great resistance to the first IMF arrangement, but participation became relatively common thereafter.

Finally, consider the effect of the number of veto players: 0.40 (*p*-value = 0.02). Even after controlling for all of the variables discussed above, the number of veto players in the political system has a statistically significant positive effect on IMF participation. To get a picture of the substantive effect of the number of veto players, consider Figure 3.6, which depicts the probability of entering into an IMF program for political systems with different numbers of veto players.

One concern about the results presented here is the small number of observations (684). The sample is small not only because we are looking only at the probability of entering into IMF programs, but also because there are so many missing observations for the economic variables of current account, foreign reserves, and debt service. Thus, Table 3.3 presents a stripped down specification leaving these variables out and including only per capita income, past participation, and number of veto players. The substantive results for these variables hold.

Conclusion

IMF programs are controversial. As the next chapter shows, IMF arrangements have strong effects on income distribution. Protest – sometimes violent protest – accompanies the onset of many of these austerity programs. Thus, the question of why so many governments participate in IMF programs is an intrinsically interesting and important one. This chapter shows that there are both economic and political reasons that governments are willing to submit to IMF conditionality. Typically, governments need a loan from the IMF because foreign reserves are low or debt is high. Yet, there are also political motivations. Governments are more likely to participate in IMF programs when other governments in the country's history have already broken the ice. Governments are also more likely to participate when they face institutionalized opposition in the form of veto players. In these cases, governments may desire IMF conditionality to help push policies past such opposition.

The IMF Articles of Agreement indicate that IMF lending should address balance of payments problems, should be temporary, and should be consistent with the broader goals of the IMF, such as promoting national prosperity. Yet, this chapter has shown that IMF programs are not strictly employed to address balance of payments problems, and they have certainly not been temporary. Have they at least promoted national prosperity? Chapter 4 shows that they have not. Before moving on to the effectiveness of IMF programs, however, one must first ask *how* to evaluate IMF programs. Evaluating the effects of IMF programs is not straightforward because of something called the "selection problem," discussed at the beginning of the next chapter.

So, besides being interesting in its own right, the question of why governments participate in IMF programs – the selection question – is also important as a means to understanding the effects of IMF programs. One cannot evaluate the effects of IMF programs without understanding the selection process. This is because one must distinguish between the circumstances that lead governments to participate in IMF programs and the inherent effects of IMF programs.

4 What are the effects of IMF programs?

In classes on international institutions like the IMF, professors rightfully encourage their students to read newspapers. Students should be knowledgeable about current events and world affairs. They should know the headlines – the *exceptional*. The evaluation of institutions like the IMF should also be based, however, on the cases that do not make the headlines, the routine cases that are so common they go unnoticed by most newspapers – the *typical*.

When evaluating the effects of a major international institution such as the IMF, one needs to be careful not to be unduly influenced by extreme cases. This is tricky business, because we are more likely to hear about extreme cases than typical cases. Newspapers are not likely to lead with headlines about the average experience of a country participating in an IMF program. The stories that get the most coverage are those that are anything but typical – this is what makes them newsworthy. Such newsworthy items, however, could lead one astray from answering important questions about the typical effects of IMF programs. Debacles, like the 2001 Argentine economic collapse,[1] and stories of notable success, such as the bailout of Mexico after its 1994 economic crisis,[2] are of historical importance and should not be forgotten. Yet, what about cases like Kenya in the early 1980s[3] or Poland in the 1990s?[4] The lessons learned from these lesser known cases may be more instructive about the "typical," "average," "expected," or "most likely" effects of IMF programs than the cases that catch attention in the news. And the expected effect – along with a gauge of how certain we are – is really what one wants to know about when asking about IMF effectiveness.

No one can predict exactly what will be the experience of a country participating in an IMF program. The relationships between policy instruments and outcomes are not precise, and there are countless intervening factors that cannot be anticipated. Yet, the question is too important to be ignored. When a government enters into an IMF program it gains access to a line of credit, and it must change – often drastically – fiscal and monetary policies. We would like to know the effects of such an economic program. When countries participate in IMF programs, we want to know what *would* have happened if they had not. When countries do not participate in IMF programs, we want to know what *would* have happened if they had. What we are after is a "counterfactual."

The problem with counterfactuals, of course, is that they cannot actually be observed. So, one must make educated guesses based on theory and evidence. The goal is to determine the typical effect along with a gauge of uncertainty, so statistical techniques are useful. Statistical models allow one to estimate the typical effect of IMF programs, controlling for – or holding constant – many other intervening factors. They also indicate whether the effect is "statistically significant," which provides a gauge of uncertainty – how much actual cases deviate from the average experience. When an effect is found not to hold statistical "significance," there is such wide variation that one cannot say that the effect is positive or negative with much degree of confidence. If an effect is statistically significant, the correlation is strong – the convention is to look for at least 95 percent confidence that the true relationship is not zero.

While statistical approaches are useful, however, there are many different statistical approaches one can employ to evaluate the effects of IMF programs, and the choice is not uncontroversial. Different techniques do not always produce the same results.

This chapter covers (in a non-technical manner) statistical techniques that have been employed to evaluate the effectiveness of IMF programs. With an understanding of why different techniques may lead to different estimations of IMF effects, the chapter then presents the results of different studies of the effects of IMF programs. There are contradictory results. Statistical results do not just present the "facts" as revealed by the data. Rather, the statistical evaluation of IMF programs is highly dependent on statistical theory.

A wealth of data

Most of what happens under IMF programs does not make newspaper headlines, and people are often surprised to learn just how common IMF programs are. Even casual examination of IMF data reveals that participation in IMF programs is business as usual for many developing countries.

The data are organized by country-years. So there is one observation for Afghanistan in 1951, followed by a second observation of Afghanistan in 1952, followed eventually by the yearly observations of Albania, Algeria, and so on up to Zimbabwe. For each country, the data for participation in IMF programs begin either in the first year of a country's independence or in 1951, whichever is later.[5] The data go up to the year 2000, although for some countries there is an earlier end-year because the country ceased to exist, like Czechoslovakia (which officially split into the Czech Republic and Slovakia on January 1, 1993), or because the country drastically changed in size, like Yugoslavia in 1991 (when Slovenia and Croatia declared their independence). In sum, the data cover 199 countries for a total of 7,132 observations.

What is remarkable about these data is the frequency of participation in conditioned IMF programs – SBA, EFF, SAF, or ESAF/PRGF arrangements. Out of the 7,132 observations, participation took place at least during part of the year in 1,838 of them. That accounts for more than 25 percent of the observations – implying that during any given year, about one quarter of the world was under an IMF program at some point. Moreover, as we learned in the last chapter, participation rates have increased over time. Countries participated in only about 9 percent of observations in the 1950s, but they participated in about 23 percent in the 1960s. In the 1970s, the relative level of participation dropped slightly to about 19 percent; this drop was due in part to the fact that countries going off of the gold standard no longer needed the IMF, and in part because of the addition of so many newly independent African countries that refrained from borrowing from the IMF.[6] In the 1980s, countries participated in IMF agreements in about 30 percent of the observations. In the 1990s, participation jumped up to 36 percent.

With this wealth of experience, one might think that there should be a pretty clear picture of just how effective these programs have been. Yet, there is not. Despite the wealth of data, evidence of program effectiveness is murky. Different statistical studies of the effects of IMF programs have arrived at different results across indicators such as balance of payments, inflation, and economic growth.

Why are there contradictory results? The reason is that evaluating the effects of IMF programs is not straightforward. Countries do not enter into IMF arrangements as random experiments. As the previous chapter shows, the circumstances of countries that participate in IMF programs differ systematically from the circumstances of countries that do not. Thus, to evaluate IMF programs, one must be able to identify what part of the outcome is due to these circumstances and what part is due to the IMF program itself. Various statistical techniques have been applied to address this problem of "nonrandom selection," and different methods sometimes lead to different results.

Thus, before addressing what different studies have found, it is important to first consider the different statistical methods that have been employed to evaluate the effects of IMF programs. The rest of this section covers the following methods: the before-after approach, the with-without approach, an approach to control for selection on observed variables, an approach to control for selection on unobserved factors, and an alternative method to control for non-random selection, called an instrumental variable approach.

The before-after approach

Early studies used a straightforward approach: average outcomes both before and after an IMF program are compared. This is the most intuitive approach. It is not unlike observing the following: Brazil entered into a SBA in 1992, which lasted until 1993; the gross domestic product (GDP) in 1991 contracted by 0.5 percent, but then grew by nearly 5 percent in 1993 and by nearly 6 percent in 1994[7] – so, one might decide that this was a successful program.

This is how one is prone to consider events as they unfold, but the approach is problematic. When comparing economic performance before and after IMF participation, one must assume that nothing else affected the country. Not only does one ignore other country-specific factors – such as economic factors, the type of government, and the motivations of political leaders – but also world conditions – such as global economic output, levels of international trade, or international lending rates. The counterfactual of what would have happened if the country had not participated in the IMF program comes entirely from what was observed before the program began. One must assume that nothing else would have changed if the IMF program had not been introduced. This is a big assumption.

Of course, even the earliest studies of IMF effectiveness were much more sophisticated than this simple example. Researchers attempted to "control" for – or hold constant – these other factors, but they were limited by the statistical techniques available at the time and the availability of data.

The with-without approach

A slightly more sophisticated, but still intuitive approach is known as "with-without": outcomes are compared between observations of IMF participation and non-participation. For observations of countries participating, the counterfactual of what would have happened had they not participated comes from what we observe in countries actually not participating.

It is not surprising that this approach shows that when countries participate in IMF programs, performance on a host of economic indicators is much worse than when countries do not participate. This is obviously because countries are much more likely to participate in IMF programs when they are facing severe economic problems. If countries turn to the IMF only when they have economic problems, this is not a fair comparison. To conclude that IMF programs hurt growth or worsen inflation from the observed negative differences is akin to concluding that doctors hurt their patients because people who go to the doctor have poorer health than people who do not. The observed difference partly reflects the circumstances that led governments to sign IMF arrangements in the first place.

Recent studies of the effects of IMF programs have made methodological advances to address these problems. The basic intuition and goal of these methods, however, follows the "with-without" way of thinking: How can one approximate what counterfactuals would look like with and without participation in IMF programs, holding the "selection" circumstances equal?

Controlling for selection on observed variables

The preceding chapters show that countries are most likely to enter into IMF programs under specific economic and political conditions: at low levels of development, when foreign reserves are low, when a country is facing domestic veto players, or when a country is favored by the United States. When controlling for selection on observed variables, one makes explicit use of this information when evaluating the effects of IMF programs.

Recall the statistical model introduced in Chapter 3. This model estimated the effects of different variables on the likelihood of participation in IMF programs. Note that the results of this estimation allow one to summarize the overall propensity of a country to participate in an IMF program. For example, the results presented in Table 3.2 of Chapter 3 indicated that when all of the variables in that specification are held to their median values, the estimated probability of entering into a spell of IMF arrangements is 0.15. For other values of the variables, the model indicates different probabilities of entering into IMF programs.

To make this very concrete, consider some examples. In 1991, the Dominican Republic had per capita income of $2,111 (1985 PPP), a current account balance of –2.07 percent of GDP, foreign reserves averaging 2.16 times monthly imports, debt service of 20.4 percent of imports, a history of previous IMF arrangements, and a score of 7 on the veto players measure. According to the estimation presented in Table 3.2 of Chapter 3, the values of these variables indicate that the overall probability of the Dominican Republic entering into an IMF arrangement during this year was about 0.34. This is quite high compared to the baseline probability of just 0.15. Chile, in 1998, faced much different circumstances: per capita income of $6,701 (1985 PPP), a current account balance of –5.25 percent of GDP, foreign reserves averaging 7.78 times monthly imports, debt service of 6.32 percent of imports, a history of previous IMF arrangements, and a score of 3 on the veto players measure. The estimated probability of Chile entering an IMF arrangement was just 0.03. Circumstances were such that the Dominican Republic in 1991 was more than ten times more likely to participate in IMF programs than Chile was in 1998 (0.34 probability versus 0.03). These are just probabilities – they do not imply that these countries actually participated, but as it turns out, the Dominican Republic actually did enter into an IMF program in 1991 and Chile did not in 1998.

One could perform this exercise for all countries during all years, producing an overall propensity score for each country-year observation.[8] What does this propensity score allow us to do? Note that within a cohort of propensity – say, the group of observations with about a 0.20 probability of participation – some of the observations will be of countries actually participating (about 20 percent of this cohort), and some of the observations will be of countries actually not participating (about 80 percent of this cohort). By comparing the performance countries within the same cohort of propensity to participate, one essentially controls for the selection problem, at least with respect to the observed variables used to estimate the probability of participation. This is a way to distinguish all of the factors that make a country likely to participate (the selection problem) from the inherent effects of the IMF program itself.

So, if one wanted to study the effects of IMF programs on economic growth, instead of simply comparing the growth of countries participating in IMF programs to the growth of countries not participating – which would surely show better performance for the countries not participating – one could compare growth across countries facing the same circumstances. Essentially, this is the same as a with-without approach, but the selection problem is accounted for, at least with respect to observed variables driving selection, and one could also control for other factors that affect economic growth but may not be related to participation in IMF programs (such as labor force growth).

The mathematics behind the propensity score may not be intuitive to all readers, but the basic idea should be clear: when using a with-without approach to evaluate the effects of the IMF, one should be careful to account for the circumstances that precipitated IMF participation – the selection circumstances.

Controlling for selection on unobserved variables

The above method to control for selection relies entirely on the observed factors driving IMF participation. Using the specification from Chapter 3, the variables are per capita income, current account balance, foreign reserves, debt service, history of previous IMF arrangements, and the number of veto players. There may be other factors that systematically influence IMF participation that have not been accounted for. Some might be readily included, but others may not be easily measured. If something that cannot be directly observed influences IMF participation and also influences economic performance, then the above method will not adequately address the selection problem.

Consider "political will" as an example. When a country fails to persevere in an IMF program, Fund officials may claim that the government lacks the "political will" to continue. As Bird notes, "The IMF has frequently blamed the poor record of the programs that it supports on a lack of 'political will' to carry them through."[9] Note that by blaming a lack of political will for program failure, one implies that countries persevering throughout a program have political will while countries that discontinue participation do not. Despite constant references to a failure of political will, however, the IMF is notoriously bad at defining exactly what the term means.[10] Some say that it is related to a government's timing of program implementation.[11] Bird conjectures that it may have something to do with the government's commitment to the program. Perhaps Fund officials are referring to the competence of the government and its advisors, or to the government's reputation, or its publicly unobserved negotiation posture with international creditors. Alternatively, it may refer to other, as yet unnamed, factors. The bottom line is that there is some factor that observers close to IMF programs – the Fund officials themselves – claim systematically determines both participation in IMF programs (perseverance) and their outcomes (program success).

This has important implications for the evaluation of the effects of IMF programs. Suppose the Fund continues signing agreements only with countries that have high levels of political will. If political will also affects economic growth, then one will overstate the effectiveness of IMF programs if one fails to control for this unobserved determinant of participation and performance. Simply that we do not observe all factors affecting selection and performance does not imply that we should ignore them.

Yet, how can we account for unobserved factors in statistical analyses of IMF effectiveness? The intuition goes as follows:

- When one estimates the probability of IMF participation, a statistical model is used that explicitly accounts for error. Sometimes the model predicts a high probability of an IMF program, even though the country did not actually participate. Sometimes the model predicts a low probability of an IMF program, even though the country did actually participate. Why do such mistakes occur? There are factors that are not accounted for – unobserved factors – that drive the participation process.
- Similarly, a statistical model can be employed to estimate the determinants of an indicator of economic performance, such as economic growth or inflation. This statistical model also explicitly accounts for error. Sometimes economic growth or inflation will be predicted either higher or lower than actually observed. Again, the reason the statistical model does not predict perfectly is that there are factors unaccounted for – unobserved factors – that drive economic performance.
- So, there are two statistical models – one of selection and one of performance – that both have explicit measures of error. These error terms may not be correlated. If they are not, then there is little reason to believe that the unobserved factors driving selection also affect performance, and there is no problem of selection on unobserved factors. Yet, suppose, on the other hand, that these errors are correlated. In other words, suppose that for country-year observations where the selection model mistakenly predicts participation, the performance model mistakenly predicts high economic growth for the same country-year observations. Then it is likely that the same unobserved factors that drive the selection process also drive economic performance. Once such a correlation is detected, one can disentangle how much of economic performance

is due to the unobserved factors driving selection and how much is due to the inherent effects of IMF programs.

For those not familiar with statistical estimation, this may seem complicated, but the intuition should be made clear. Just like controlling for selection on observed factors, one attempts to compare observations that are similar in every respect – except IMF participation status – to estimate the counterfactual of what would have occurred in the absence/presence of an IMF program. Here, one explicitly tries to control for the unobserved factors driving both selection into IMF programs and IMF program effectiveness by taking advantage of the feature of all statistical models: the error term. One controls for the correlation between the errors in selection and the errors in performance.

Controlling for the correlation between the error terms of selection into IMF programs and IMF effects probably sounds daunting to most readers. It should! The statistical method relies on important assumptions about errors, such as that they are symmetrically distributed. We typically assume that error terms follow the normal, or bell-shaped, distribution. If this assumption is violated, however, then the statistical model may produce biased estimates of IMF program effects. Thus, other methods have been proposed.

Instrumental variables

Ideally, instead of trying to correct for nonrandom selection, a researcher could perform experiments. The IMF, of course, does not engage in random experiments with respect to IMF programs. What if, however, there were some rule of thumb the IMF followed when imposing IMF programs on countries that is random with respect to the economic circumstances and impacts of IMF programs? One could then assume that, to the extent this seemingly arbitrary rule of thumb drives IMF participation, there exists a sort of "natural experiment."

The previous chapter showed that much of what explains IMF participation is economic – but there are also some other factors that may be unrelated to economic circumstances, such as some of the international political factors discussed in Chapter 2, that also determine selection into IMF programs.

An instrumental variables approach involves finding some factor that drives selection into IMF programs, but does not affect the outcome that one is trying to evaluate. For example, suppose that countries with many citizens working at the IMF are more likely to get a loan from the IMF, due to better connections through the IMF bureaucracy, but having a lot of citizens working at the IMF has nothing to do with the year to year economic growth of the country. Then, one may be able to use this variable to gain leverage over the problem of distinguishing selection from growth. Controlling for many other factors, economic growth should be random with respect to the number of citizens working at the IMF. Again, it is as if the world has produced a natural experiment. Some countries (those with lots of citizens working at the IMF) are randomly assigned to participate in an IMF program, while other countries (those with few citizens working at the IMF) are randomly assigned to not participate in an IMF program. Then the difference in economic growth can be assumed to be due entirely to the inherent effect of IMF programs.

The elusive key with this method is finding this "instrumental variable." The problem with the variables listed in this section above is that even though they may not be related to the economic impacts of IMF programs, they may be intrinsically related to the *design* of IMF programs. Countries with connections to the IMF, political or otherwise, may be more likely not just to get an IMF loan, but also to get softer conditions. Using such variables as instruments to control for nonrandom selection may lead to biased results because the programs for countries with connections to the IMF may be systematically different from programs with countries that lack such connections. Moreover, not only does the instrumental variable approach require imagination to come up with the elusive instrument, one must also be able to get data on the instrumental variable. Beyond this, one must take care to hold constant many other factors that actually do affect both IMF participation and IMF outcomes in a systematic – or non-random – way.

True experimentation?

The methods described here are not uncontroversial. The simple methods, such as before-after and with-without, have obvious drawbacks because they ignore the selection problem. Yet, the more sophisticated methods that attempt to control for the selection problem rely heavily on assumptions about how errors are distributed. Instrumental variables can address this problem, but they are not easy to come by, especially since so much of what drives selection into IMF programs also influences IMF program effects. Thus, evaluations of the effects of IMF programs are not straightforward.

Yet, the questions of how IMF programs impact economic growth, inflation, balance of payments, income distribution, poverty, the environment, and social spending are important and must be addressed. We need to consider counterfactual questions of what would have happened in countries that participated in IMF programs had they not, and what would have happened in countries that did not participate in IMF program if they had. Since one cannot observe these counterfactual states, the best way to get a picture of what they would look like is through careful comparison. In the absence of carefully controlled experiments, statistical models provide a set of tools by which to perform comparisons across the wealth of data that 1,838 cumulative country-years of experience under IMF programs provides.

Before moving on to what researchers have found using different statistical techniques, it is worthwhile to pause for a moment to imagine what one would learn from truly experimental data. Field experimentation would be a powerful method for drawing inferences about the effect of IMF programs. The experimenter would randomly assign some countries to participate in an IMF program and other countries not to participate. If these "treatment" and "control" groups were randomly assigned, one could readily compare the two groups without the need for very complicated statistical models. Selection bias would not be a problem, since selection would be random, and any significant difference between the outcomes of the two groups would be due to the IMF program. The advantage of an experimental design is that even rudimentary data analysis would reveal the effect of IMF programs.

IMF officials would object to such experimentation. Advocates of experimental approaches acknowledge that policy makers may only be willing to engage in experimental design if they are indifferent between alternative approaches. The decision-makers at the IMF do not, of course, believe they operate according to arbitrary rules. They are trained economists who have a canon of theories with which they approach the world. Thus, they are unwilling to experiment, especially since such an experiment would negatively impact millions of people. In an experiment, one of the two groups of countries – the treatment or the control group – would suffer if IMF programs have any effect. If IMF programs have beneficial consequences, the control group would suffer; if programs have negative consequences, the treatment group would suffer.

To put this in context, consider the effects IMF programs may have on economic growth. If IMF programs systematically impact economic growth, then one of the groups would experience lower growth than the other. Unlucky countries would be assigned to the group that produces worse results. This unlucky group would suffer from lower rates of economic growth, which could result in a plethora of negative outcomes associated with lower income: lower standards of living, less stable democracy, more civil unrest, less education, more wars, more children dying, and the list goes on. The detrimental consequences of policies that hurt economic growth should not be understated.

Hence, many people reach the conclusion that experimentation with IMF programs is unethical. How unfair it would be to subject millions of people to an experiment where one group would suffer more than the other. Just thinking about experimentation, however, highlights a sad situation: at present, there is controversy over which of the two groups – the treatment group or the control group – would be the lucky one. As presented below, different studies have reached different conclusions with respect to the effects of IMF programs on balance of payments, inflation, and economic growth, as well as income distribution, social spending, and the environment. As unethical as IMF experimentation may seem, how ethical is it to prescribe a medicine whose effects are unknown?

The effects of IMF programs on the balance of payments

If IMF programs have any effect, it should be on the balance of payments (BOP). First and foremost, the Articles of Agreement mandate the IMF to address problems in this area. What is the balance of payments? The IMF defines a country's overall balance of payments as the sum of the "current account," the "capital account," and the "financial account" plus "net errors and omissions." The *current account* of the balance of payments is the credits minus the debits of goods, services, income, and current transfers. The *capital account* refers mainly to transfers of fixed assets and nonproduced, nonfinancial assets. The *financial account* is the net sum of the balance of direct investment, portfolio investment and other investment transactions. *Net errors and omissions* reflect statistical inconsistencies in the recording of entries and are included so that all debit and credit entries in the balance of payments statement sum to zero. By construction (of net errors and omissions), the overall balance of payments is equal to net changes in "reserves and related items," the sum of transactions in reserve assets, exceptional financing, and use of Fund credit and loans.[12]

Many studies have looked at the effect of IMF programs on both the overall BOP and the current account component of the BOP. The IMF mandate to address BOP problems has been clear throughout its history. The Articles of Agreement are explicit that IMF lending should go to countries experiencing BOP problems. The deficit country is taking in more imports or fixed assets or finance than it is generating through exports – the immediate purpose of an IMF arrangement is to provide a loan so that foreign debts can continue to be serviced and necessary imports can be purchased. The loan is intended to soften the blow as adjustments are made as the demand for imports and foreign financing is cut. Demand can be addressed in many ways: devaluation, where the demand for imports is cut by effectively raising their domestic price; the reduction of money supply by raising interest rates or limiting credit creation; and fiscal austerity, where governments reduce consumption both by raising taxes and by spending less. Yet it is not obvious that the IMF program will help. If governments fail to comply with IMF policy conditions, or if the IMF policies are not sufficient, BOP problems can persist. Indeed, if the IMF program causes a drastic contraction of the economy, it is possible for the BOP situation to worsen.

What have studies found? The broad consensus is that the IMF has had success in addressing balance of payments problems.[13] For example, in an early study conducted by economist and professor of Latino Studies at the University of California, Santa Cruz, Manuel Pastor, IMF programs were found to have a positive, statistically significant effect on the BOP, using a before-after methodology analyzing Latin American countries during 1965–1981.[14] Another early study using a before-after approach to study Latin America, by Tony Killick, along with colleagues Moazzam Malik and Marcus Manuel, also found a statistically significant positive effect of IMF programs on the BOP.[15] Using a with-without methodology to analyze 32 programs implemented during 1977–1979, Thorvaldur Gylfason, a former IMF economist and current professor at the University of Iceland, also found a positive effect of IMF programs on the BOP.[16] In a more expansive with-without study of 69 countries from 1973 to 1988, Mohsin Khan, who is currently the director of the IMF Institute, also found a statistically significant positive impact of IMF programs on the BOP.[17] Khan also employed a method controlling for nonrandom selection on observed variables to the same data and found the same positive significant effect.

Many of these studies also find that IMF programs have a positive significant impact on the current account of the BOP in particular. Khan finds this using before-after, with-without, and approaches dealing with nonrandom selection; Killick, Malik, and Manuel find it using a before-after approach; and another widely-cited study by Patrick Conway, economist at the University of North Carolina, finds a positive significant impact of IMF programs on the current account using a sophisticated approach controlling for nonrandom selection on observed variables.[18]

A notable exception to the consensus that IMF programs improve the BOP is a study conducted by IMF economists Morris Goldstein and Peter Montiel.[19] They actually find a negative impact using before-after, with-without, and approaches dealing with nonrandom selection, but the finding is not statistically significant. In fact, no study cited in the literature finds a statistically significant negative effect of IMF programs on the BOP.[20]

So, while there are exceptions, most studies have found that IMF programs have a positive impact on the BOP. This finding is supported across various methodologies and data sets. This is not so for other areas of interest. In these other areas – where the IMF has failed (discussed below) – people debate whether the IMF has failed because it prescribes bad policies or because countries have failed to comply with IMF arrangements. When it comes to the BOP, there is no debate in the literature over why the IMF has the impact that it does. It is simply assumed to be the result of governments following IMF policy conditions. It seems that when it comes to an area of success, the compliance question is not raised. It should be, however. Presumably, if IMF programs have a significant impact on the BOP, governments must be adjusting. They must be complying with IMF programs – unless the IMF loan itself is enough to stabilize the country.

Inflation and budget deficits

When looking for evidence of compliance, analysts often study policy areas where governments exert a great deal of control, such as fiscal or monetary policy.[21] Hence, research addresses budget deficits and inflation. The far and away majority of IMF programs contain policies (discussed above) that should have a direct impact on these areas. What has the literature found to be the impact of IMF programs?

Regarding the fiscal adjustment, which a recent report of the IMF Independent Evaluation Office (IEO) notes is "widely regarded as one of the core elements of macroeconomic design in IMF-supported programs,"[22] the IMF appears to have an effect. According to Killick, Malik and Manuel's before-after study of 16 countries from 1979 to 1985, IMF programs have a positive effect on the overall budget balance. This finding was confirmed using a more sophisticated statistical technique to control for nonrandom selection on observed variables in Conway's 1994 study of 74 countries from 1976 to 1986. Conway found the IMF has a positive statistically significant effect on budget surplus. Yet, the IMF IEO 2003 study reports that there is a great deal of variation. On average, deficits are indeed reduced, but "fiscal balances improved by half the projected amounts."[23] So even if IMF programs have a positive effect on the budget deficit, there appears to be a problem with compliance. This is something the following chapter addresses. It is important to point out here, however, that the IEO report notes that despite the widely held belief that IMF programs always involve fiscal austerity, about one-third of the arrangements they examined called for the fiscal deficit to widen. This is most likely because their data cover a more recent period (1993–2001) than previous analyses. This may reflect a more pro-poor attitude the IMF has taken since the late 1990s.

The evidence regarding the effect of IMF programs on inflation is even murkier. In his work, Randall Stone reviews 22 studies of the effect of IMF programs on inflation, which use different methodologies, cover various data sets, and were published as far back as 1978 and as recently as 2000. There appears to be no consensus. Six studies report no effect; ten studies report that inflation falls but the effect is not statistically significant; three studies report a statistically significant negative effect, and three studies report that inflation actually rises, though the effect is not statistically significant. The studies that found a significant negative effect were older and used early before-after and with-without methodology. Using sophisticated methodology controlling for nonrandom selection, no significant effect was found.

This implies that either IMF policies do not effectively address inflation, or that governments fail to comply with IMF policies (or both). Which is it? The next chapter, on compliance, discusses this question in detail. Here, it is important to note that in his research on Eastern Europe in the 1990s, Randall Stone finds that the problem is compliance. When he looks specifically at countries that the IMF did not punish for noncompliance, he finds a statistically significant effect of IMF programs curtailing inflation. His results are promising, but no one has applied his methodology to other regions or time periods. The consensus on the effects of IMF programs on inflation thus remain tentative, although some are optimistic that with better compliance, IMF programs can have more of an effect in this area.

Economic growth

What is the effect of IMF programs on economic development? For some, this is the most important question. Sustainable economic development and prosperity address many of the other economic problems discussed above. An economy that is growing can avoid or afford to sustain BOP and fiscal deficits, and can afford to maintain some degree of inflation. Economic development is also associated with numerous important indicators of quality of life for people. Some argue, however, that economic growth is not and should not be a goal of the IMF. They point out that the original purpose of the IMF was to address balance of payments problems and that the focus on economic growth is something that developed over time. The claim is that the IMF was never intended to promote economic growth.

Yet, this is not completely true. The Articles of Agreement call upon the IMF to provide members "with opportunity to correct maladjustments in their balance of payments *without resorting to measures destructive of national or international prosperity*" [emphasis added]. This certainly indicates that the IMF should at least not hurt prospects for economic growth.

The Report of the Executive Directors for the First Annual Meeting of the Board of Governors in 1946 was even more explicit:

> The function of the Fund is to aid members in maintaining arrangements that promote the balanced expansion of international trade and investment and in this way *contribute to the maintenance of high levels of employment and real income.*[24]

Right from the first meeting of the governing body of the IMF, high levels of employment and income were central.

Even though the IMF shifted its focus from the industrialized world to the developing world, the importance of promoting national prosperity remained. In fact, the IMF has become increasingly concerned with promoting growth and addressing poverty over time. As Michel Camdessus, the IMF Managing Director from 1987 to 2000, described,

> Our primary objective is growth ... It is toward growth that our programs and their conditionality are aimed. It is with a view toward growth that we carry out our special responsibility of helping to correct balance of payments disequilibria and, more generally, to eliminate obstructive macroeconomic imbalances. When I refer to growth, I mean high-quality growth, not ... growth for the privileged few, leaving the poor with nothing but empty promises.

Managing Director Horst Köhler, who took the helm at the IMF after Camdessus, emphasized the importance of promoting world financial stability, but he also echoed the views of his predecessor, contending that "the IMF should strive to promote non-inflationary economic growth that benefits all people of the world."[25]

How effective has the IMF been at promoting economic growth? Not very. Not only is evidence of growth promotion weak, recent studies even show that IMF programs have a significant *negative* effect on economic growth. Early studies consistently showed no statistically significant effect. Out of nine before-after studies from 1978 to 1995, covering different countries, regions, and time spans, only one reported a significant positive effect.[26] Four of the others reported no effect; two reported a statistically insignificant negative effect; and one reported an insignificant positive effect. Using with-without comparisons, results were similar – some show insignificant positive effects, others insignificant negative effects, still others show no effect at all, but none of them show a statistically significant effect.

With more sophisticated methodology, new results emerged. Khan's 1990 study, which addressed nonrandom selection, showed a significant negative effect on growth in the short run, with the adverse effects on growth diminishing thereafter. In his study published in 1994, Conway built upon this result using an advanced technique to control for nonrandom selection on observed variables. He showed that IMF programs have an initial significant negative effect on growth, but a significant *positive* effect within three years. The take-away point of Conway's study is that IMF programs start out badly but end well.

The Conway study had a profound impact. The result made a lot of sense. As IMF economists Nadeem Ul Haque and Mohsin Khan reported in 1998: "In the case of growth, the consensus seems to be that output will be depressed in the short run as the demand-reducing elements of the policy package dominate. Over time the structural reform elements of the program start to take effect and growth begins to rise."[27] A subsequent study by IMF economists Louis Dicks-Mireaux, Mauro Mecagni, and Susan Schadler provided further evidence, showing that ESAF programs from the 1986–1991 period appeared to have a statistically significant positive effect on output growth.[28] This study used an advanced methodology to deal with the selection problem. It then went further, however, by testing some of the statistical assumptions underlying the model. They found that many of the assumptions were dubious, and this caused them to raise doubts about the reliability of the statistical findings.

Then a series of studies found a statistically significant negative effect on growth, using similarly advanced statistical techniques. The 2000 study by political scientist Adam Przeworski and me controlled for nonrandom selection on unobserved variables like "political will" and "trust." The analysis on 79 countries from 1971 to 1990 showed a statistically significant negative effect on annual output growth of about 1.5 percent. Similar results were obtained on a larger sample including 135 countries from 1951 to 1990. No evidence of a long run positive effect was found.[29]

In their 2003 study of Latin America, economists Michael Hutchison of University of California, Santa Cruz, and Ilan Noy of University of Hawaii show that IMF programs have a negative effect on economic growth. In fact, they show that the effect is worse for countries that "successfully" complete programs.[30] This raises an important point that is addressed in the next chapter on compliance: even – indeed, *especially* – countries that complete IMF programs experience lower growth.

In their study, published in 2005, economists Robert Barro and Jong-Wha Lee also found disappointing results. Using an instrumental variable approach to address the selection problem, they found that IMF programs have a negative effect in the short run that is not statistically significant, and a strong statistically significant *negative* effect on economic growth in the long run.[31] This result runs directly counter to the consensus described by Haque and Khan in 1998. Finally, in a study published in 2006 that also uses an instrumental variables approach to the selection problem, economist Axel Dreher further confirms that IMF programs lower growth – his results also deal with compliance and are discussed in the next chapter.[32] Dreher finds that compliance somewhat mitigates this effect, but even for countries that comply the effect is negative.

So, the newly emerging consensus is that IMF programs hurt economic growth. The initial contractionary effect of IMF programs is really not surprising. Some economists at the IMF have been quite forthright about why. IMF economist Vito Tanzi, for example, has argued that IMF programs induce governments to save on public investment, with nefarious consequences for growth.[33] IMF economists Mario Blejer and Adrienne Cheasty point out that the high real interest rates induce good firms to shut down along with bad ones, which can also hurt growth. Plus, there is the straightforward effect of IMF austerity cutting demand, which drives down economic growth. As for the failure to promote long run growth, the fact that the "economic stabilization" induced by IMF programs does not eventually lead to improved economic growth is disappointing, but also not surprising. The IMF insists that macroeconomic stability is necessary for economic growth. This may be true, but it is not sufficient. There is no theory that says a balanced budget, a balance of payments, and low inflation should induce economic growth. Moreover, it appears that programs that stabilize inflation, reduce deficits, improve the balance of payments, and at the same time do not *hurt* growth, are yet to be developed.

Income distribution and social spending

It is notable that studies of the effect of IMF programs on BOP, budget deficits, inflation, and growth reach different conclusions, depending on the methodology and data employed. This is not so with respect to income distribution. There have been three studies using three different methodologies and three different data sets. All come to the same conclusion: typically, IMF programs exacerbate income inequality.

Pastor conducted the first study in 1987, using the before-after approach to analyze labor's share of income in Latin America during 1965–1981. His conclusion was strong: "The single most consistent effect the IMF seems to have is the redistribution of income away from workers."[34] Pastor's study was path breaking, but the early study was limited by the methodology, which did not account for nonrandom selection, and because it looked only at Latin America. These limitations were addressed by a young scholar at Harvard University, Gopal Garuda, who published in 2000 his study of the effect of IMF programs on overall income distribution.[35] Garuda looked at a standard index of overall income inequality called the "Gini coefficient."[36] He addressed the selection problem by estimating the propensity of countries to participate in IMF programs, using a statistical model similar to the one presented in Chapter 3. Then he compared countries with and without IMF programs that had similar circumstances or "propensities" to participate in IMF programs. One interesting new finding Garuda discovered is that when countries unlikely to participate in IMF programs do participate, income inequality does not increase. However, for countries that are likely to participate, IMF programs exacerbate income inequality. The Garuda study was limited by the small amount of data on Gini coefficients that are available – this is why he incorporated a selection model within a with-without framework. He did not have enough data to employ a standard selection model.

In a study I published in 2002, the limited data problem was resolved by just looking at the manufacturing sector of the economy. The data on labor's share of earnings from manufacturing are available for 2,095 observations of 110 countries from 1961 to 1993. With these data, a fully parameterized selection model is possible. The result of the study confirmed the two it built upon: IMF programs increase income inequality.[37]

The empirics on this question are important because it is not obvious from a theoretical point of view what the effect of IMF programs will be on income inequality. IMF programs include many policy changes that can potentially influence the distribution of income in various ways. Yet, the direction and magnitude of the effects depend on particular characteristics of the economy and the details of how reforms are structured. Economists at the Fund have claimed "the distributional effects of IMF stabilization programs are so complex that they defy simple categorization."[38]

Devaluation, for example, decreases the price ratio of nontradable to tradable goods. If the poor are rural farmers producing goods for exports, this can improve the distribution of income, but if the poor are urban consumers facing higher food prices, it can increase income inequality.[39] Devaluation can also worsen the distribution of income if elite groups engage in capital flight prior to the devaluation.[40] Reducing access to domestic credit, by increasing interest rates or bank reserve requirements, or by imposing explicit credit ceilings, affects groups according to their access to other sources of credit. In an early study, IMF economists Omotunde Johnson and Joanne Salop point out that large, well-established firms are favored over small and medium sized firms, and the urban sector is favored over the rural sector.[41] Reduction of public expenditure can also have an effect. As Johnson and Salop note, "the brunt of any downward adjustment of government expenditure to GDP is most commonly borne out by public sector employees engaged in projects that come to be post-poned, together with the private domestic suppliers of services associated with such projects. These tend to be highly capital-intensive ventures in construction and public utilities."[42] Wage freezes, limits on employment, and reduced benefits for public employees are also common. The overall effect of reducing the government budget deficit on income distribution depends on the composition of the budget cuts, the mobility of producers, and the adaptability of consumer patterns. As Garuda explains, "virtually any overall result can be achieved, provided that overall expenditures are reduced."[43]

Because programs can be achieved in many different ways with different consequences for distribution, study after study has noted that the political power of various groups may influence the final outcome. The fact that IMF programs appear to have the systematic effect of increasing income inequality indicates that governments may use the leverage of the IMF to push through reform policies in such a way to insulate elite constituencies and force the costs of adjustment on labor and the poor. As Johnson and Salop note, "Domestic political considerations will largely determine who bears the burden of reducing and restructuring aggregate demand," and "the choice of policy instruments will be influenced by the political power of various income groups."[44]

There are some interesting nuances in the literature on the effects of IMF programs on the poor that are worth noting. For example, New York University professor and former World Bank economist William Easterly found that IMF and World Bank programs mute the effects of economic growth on the poor.[45] This is good when growth is hurt, as the contraction hurts them less; but it is unfortunate when the economy expands, because the growth does not reach them. This may indicate that the poor are simply less integrated into the formal sector of the economy, and are not affected by changes in monetary and fiscal policy. The burden may be heaviest on the poor that are integrated into the formal economy and on labor.

How do IMF programs impact government spending on programs that should impact the poor, such as spending on health and education? Two recent reports from the IMF Independent Evaluation Office (IEO) indicate that IMF programs do not force governments to cut such spending.[46] They even indicate that IMF programs may influence governments to spend more on health and education.

The 2003 IEO study, conducted under IEO economist Marcelo Selowsky, finds that after controlling for nonrandom selection into IMF programs – the fact that countries come to the IMF under bad economic circumstances where budgets may have to be cut regardless of IMF participation – the inherent effect of IMF programs is to increase spending on education and health. The study is comprehensive, considering 146 countries from 1985 to 2000. The 2004 IEO study conducted by IEO economists Ricardo Martin and Alex Segura-Ubiergo further confirmed this finding.[47]

According, however, to political scientists Irfan Nooruddin of Ohio State University and Joel W. Simmons of Michigan University, the IEO report fails to account for domestic politics. They find, first of all, that while the overall impact of IMF programs on health and education spending is positive, the effect is not statistically significant. Second, it turns out that the aggregate effect does not hold for all regime types. Under dictatorship, where spending on health and education is small, the IMF indeed has a positive effect, although spending levels remain well below democracy levels. For democracies, however, the effect is the opposite. IMF programs have a statistically significant negative effect on health and education expenditures for democracies. Taken together, IMF programs make the two regime types look similar. IMF programs make democracies look more like dictatorships when it comes to health and education. Nooruddin and Simmons conclude that optimism about the IMF successfully helping the poor "is out of place."[48]

Conclusion

Evaluating the effects of IMF programs is analogous to evaluating the effects of medical treatments. If one were to compare the health of people undergoing medical treatment to people not, one might come to the quick conclusion that medical treatments hurt patients, because they are much less healthy than the rest of the population. This is obviously because people only go to the doctor when they are sick. Yet, some medical treatments have been found to be helpful, while others are benign or even malignant. Before coming to such conclusions, one must address the selection problem – under what circumstances is treatment applied?

Researchers have addressed the selection problem when analyzing the effects of IMF programs in various ways with increasing degrees of sophistication. Nevertheless, the conclusions in the literature are tentative. With each generation of studies come new and often contradictory findings.

According to the most recent studies and reviews, the IMF seems to be most effective in addressing balance of payments problems. It is less effective in addressing inflation. And recent studies show pernicious effects on economic growth. IMF programs exacerbate income inequality according to all studies that look directly at this question. In the area of social spending, the most recent study shows that spending on health and education may increase in dictatorships, where little is spent to begin with, but IMF programs make democracies that participate in IMF programs look more like dictatorships when it comes to spending on the poor.

5 Do governments comply with IMF programs?

So far, this book has addressed why countries participate in IMF arrangements and with what effects. This chapter introduces the compliance question: Do governments live up to the promises they make when entering into IMF arrangements? When they do not, why do they fail?[1]

Compliance questions turn out to be difficult to answer for various reasons. First, until recently, most of the details of IMF arrangements were secret, so outsiders could not know for sure if countries complied or not. Second, even when information is available, it is not obvious how to define or measure compliance. Yet, the compliance question is too important to ignore. Compliance is not only intrinsically interesting, it is also necessary to address before one can turn to the question of IMF reform in the next chapter. To see why, consider the following:

Most studies of the determinants and consequences of IMF arrangements have employed a simple approach: either a country is participating or it is not. Among many other effects, these studies find that IMF programs have a negative impact on economic growth, even after one accounts for the circumstance that lead countries to enter into IMF arrangements in the first place. This begs an obvious question: Why do IMF programs hurt growth?

Consider a potential answer to this question from the *left* of the political spectrum: the negative effect of the IMF on economic growth is due to the austere economic policies the Fund imposes. Rather than allow governments to "prime the pump" during an economic crisis, the IMF attacks excess demand by encouraging governments to cut public spending, raise taxes, place a ceiling on credit creation, raise interest rates, and perhaps devalue currency. These are obviously contractionary policies – notably these are *not* the kind of policies that developed countries follow when they face economic difficulties. Rather than foster development, IMF policies curtail economic growth, which in turn may exacerbate the economic problems that led to the economic crisis in the first place – hence the need to return to the IMF again and again.

Note that this critique assumes that governments actually *comply* with policies imposed through IMF programs. It assumes that the negative effects that IMF programs have on economic growth come from the policy prescriptions of the IMF. Yet, what if governments do not actually comply with IMF programs?

This opens the door to the critique from the *right*: the problem with IMF programs is not the policy conditions but the loans. Perhaps the policy conditions that the IMF imposes are the correct ones. Indeed, if a country has gotten itself into a severe balance of payments deficit or an excessive debt problem, consumer demand should be curtailed by bringing about fiscal responsibility and tight monetary policy. These prudent policies will bring about desperately needed economic stability, which in turn sets the stage for renewed, stable economic growth. But since governments do not comply with the policy conditions, IMF programs do not help make the necessary policy adjustments. Instead, the loan that a government receives through the IMF arrangement simply subsidizes the bad policies that got the country into the economic crisis in the first place. The mechanism by which IMF programs hurt economic growth may be through the IMF loan itself, not the policy conditions prescribed by the Fund.

At the crux of this debate is the question of compliance. If IMF programs hurt economic growth when countries comply, then the critique from the left gains support: IMF programs hurt growth through bad policy advice. If IMF programs hurt economic growth when countries fail to comply, then the critique from the right gains support: IMF programs hurt growth through the loans by subsidizing bad policy.[2] To settle this debate, analysis of the compliance question is required. One must distinguish between the effects of IMF loans and the effects of IMF conditions by measuring compliance.

Thus this chapter delves into the question of compliance. First, the various methods of measuring compliance are discussed. Then findings on the causes and consequences of compliance are reviewed. The good news and bad news about this chapter is that it raises more questions than it answers. This is good news in that it represents the frontier of research on the IMF and so may prove provocative for students of the IMF interested in pursuing their own new research on IMF programs. This is bad news because it would be nice to have satisfying answers to the compliance question. The most this chapter can offer, however, is a presentation of the limited evidence that exists, and an explanation of just why compliance is so difficult to gauge.

Measuring compliance

Researchers both in universities and at the IMF have long grappled with the question of compliance, but measuring compliance is not straightforward. The study of compliance with IMF programs was originally fraught with difficulties because – until the aftermath of the East Asian financial crisis of the late 1990s – the details of most IMF programs were confidential. To get around this obstacle, researchers employed various proxies for compliance, but they are not fully satisfactory. In the new era of "transparency," better data are becoming available. The IMF makes at least some portions of all IMF arrangements publicly available through the IMF web site at www.imf.org. This has opened the door to new possibilities for studying compliance.

Data availability not withstanding, there are basically two approaches to measuring compliance: aggregate indices and disaggregated approaches. Each way has pros and cons.

The advantage of the aggregate approach is that it provides one overall indicator to settle the compliance debate. The problem with this approach is a problem that plagues many overall indices: How should weights be assigned to various components? Recall that IMF policy conditions span many dimensions: the budget deficit, interest rates, currency valuations, and structural conditions. Many of these dimensions can be broken down even further. The budget deficit can be analyzed in terms of various forms of taxation and various forms of expenditure. It is rare that a country satisfies all of the policy conditions in an IMF arrangement, but it is also atypical for a country to meet none of them. There is no clear way to compare across different policy dimensions, and it is not obvious that one should.

With disaggregate approaches, one does not attempt to compare across policy dimensions. Instead of coming up with an overall measure of compliance, one looks at compliance within one policy area, such as the interest rate or the budget deficit. Compliance rates across different policy dimensions may be quite different, and may have quite different causes and effects. Note that such an approach would lead to quite different research on IMF arrangements than what has been presented in this book. Instead of looking at the overall effect of IMF arrangements, researchers would look at the effects of specific policies under IMF arrangements. There is not much research of this kind, but this chapter discusses some of what does exist. Before proceeding, however, this chapter first presents the bulk of work on the question of compliance, which has relied on aggregate indices.

Aggregate approaches to measuring compliance

The most basic and most common measure of compliance is the percentage of the IMF loan that is used or "drawn" by a country. The logic of this measure is as follows: under a conditioned IMF arrangement (SBA, EFF, SAF, or ESAF/PRGF), a government only receives disbursements of the loan if the IMF staff and management determine that the government is in compliance with the conditions laid out in the Letter of Intent. Typically, only about 25 percent of the total loan is provided upon the approval of the arrangement. So if a government has drawn more than 25 percent of the loan, one can assume some degree of compliance with the arrangement policy conditions. If the government draws less than 100 percent of the loan, however, one can assume some degree of noncompliance.

The measure is clever in several respects. First, it gets around the problem of IMF secrecy. One does not need to know the specific policy conditions to determine compliance. Instead, one simply relies upon observable actions of the IMF, trusting the Fund to interrupt disbursements as a consequence of non-compliance. Second, the approach produces a useful aggregate measure that gets around the multidimensionality of IMF policy conditions, again by relying on the IMF's assessment of the overall degree of compliance. Third, the measure is readily available – these data are in the public domain.

Killick was the first to use this measure.[3] He created a dichotomous measure of compliance, coding arrangements where at least 80 percent of the loan was drawn upon as "compliant," and coding arrangements where less than 80 percent of the loan was drawn upon as "noncompliant." He considered 305 EFF and SAF programs from the period of 1979 to 1993.[4] By this measure, 47 percent of the arrangements studied were cases of compliance. It should be noted that Killick tested the reliability of his approach to coding compliance by comparing his index to 48 in-depth case studies from the 1980s – "The outcomes matched almost perfectly."[5]

Despite its advantages, there are several problems with this measure: first of all, the measure assumes that the only reason that countries do not draw 100 percent of the loan is noncompliance. This is a bad assumption. Sometimes IMF arrangements are precautionary. Governments may enter into an IMF arrangement just in case they need a loan. But if that need does not materialize, the government may decide not to draw upon the loan, even if the government is in compliance and could draw if it wanted to.

Governments may even enter into IMF programs not because they want a loan, per se, but rather because they actually want the IMF policy conditions to be imposed. They may want to send a signal to creditors that they have an IMF program in place and in good standing, or they may seek the leverage of the IMF as an international ally to pressure domestic opponents to policy change. Again in these situations, governments may choose not to draw on the IMF loan, even though the IMF deems the country to be in compliance.

This is a problem for the measure because fully compliant countries can be coded as noncompliant, but it is not a fatal flaw. It is possible to distinguish between countries that did not draw upon an IMF loan due to noncompliance and countries that did not use the IMF loan due to non-need.[6] But there are further problems with this approach to measuring noncompliance.

A second problem with the measure, which is remediable, has to do with the phasing of disbursements. Often countries face compliance problems early on in their arrangements. Subsequently, they get back on track, although sometimes this is after waivers on some conditions are granted. At the end of the arrangement, the full loan may eventually be disbursed, but there may have been severe compliance problems along the way. Axel Dreher has proposed a solution to this problem. He measures actual disbursements relative to equal phasing of the loan over the entire course of an arrangement. To the extent that actual disbursements deviate from an even distribution of the loan over time, compliance problems can be assumed. For example, if more than half of a loan is disbursed during the second year of a two-year arrangement, then there must have been an interruption during the first year.[7]

A more severe problem with this measure is its reliance on IMF judgment. The measure assumes that if the IMF disburses high levels of the loan, the government must be living up to the Letter of Intent. But what if international politics plays a role in the ultimate decisions of the IMF? As Chapter 2 discusses, powerful countries – mainly the United States – may pressure the IMF to treat strategically important allies more favorably than other countries. In his work on Eastern Europe and Africa, Randall Stone has shown that the IMF tends to be fairly consistent and technocratic when initially punishing a country that has failed to live up to the policy conditions in the Letter of Intent. That is, he shows economic variables predict the onset of punishment fairly well, while international politics seems not to play much of a role. Instead, he finds that international politics does play a strong role in the *duration* of punishment. Countries favored by the United States tend to get shorter punishment intervals than countries not particularly favored. The shorter punishment intervals imply that countries favored by the US may receive a larger proportion of an IMF loan than a country with a similar level of compliance/noncompliance that is not favored by the US. If this is the case, the IMF may allow some governments to draw 100 percent of the loan, even if the government fails to comply with policy conditions. Noncompliant countries may be coded as compliant.

If the *onset* of punishment is driven by economic variables, then perhaps looking directly at the initial suspension of a loan disbursement is a better approach. Susan Schadler and her colleagues at the IMF, for example, consider the quarterly reviews of IMF programs, coding noncompliance as situations where performance criteria were not met and the loan was suspended.[8] They coded 59 SBA and EFF arrangements from 1988 to 1991 and found that the IMF suspended loan disbursements in 35 cases (nearly 60 percent of cases).[9] Political scientist Martin Edwards of Texas Tech University uses a similar approach for a much broader set of agreements – 347 arrangements from 1979 to 1997 – coding noncompliance when the IMF declares a country ineligible for drawings.[10] He finds lower rates of noncompliance: 138 cases, about 40 percent.

A related approach is to consider "irreversible interruptions," defined as occurring when "either the last scheduled program review was not completed, or all scheduled reviews were completed but the subsequent annual arrangement was not approved." This measure was introduced by researchers at the IMF.[11] Using this approach to analyze 197 IMF arrangements during the 1992–2002 period, 41 percent experience an irreversible interruption. So with this measure, compliance rates are nearly 60 percent.

According to all aggregate measures, therefore, compliance is far from one hundred percent, but noncompliance is punished in some cases and rates of compliance are nontrivial, ranging from 40 to 60 percent of cases, depending on the measure employed. Yet all of the above approaches to measuring compliance suffer from a third problem: they conflate different forms of compliance into one index. This is a severe problem, and it is impossible to avoid with any aggregate approach. To understand what is at stake, consider the following:

Different IMF arrangements have different policy conditions. And even if all arrangements had the same conditions, different governments achieve various levels of compliance across the various policy dimensions covered by the arrangement. Yet, when using an aggregate index of compliance, hundreds of possible policy combinations must be conflated into one index. Countries that make great progress in tightening monetary policy may be granted continued disbursements of the IMF arrangement loan, even though the government failed to raise taxes or reduce expenditures. Another government may successfully achieve fiscal balance, but fail to privatize the telecommunications industry and fail to reform the pension system, and the IMF loan may be withheld. Sometimes the IMF calls for "prior actions" to be taken before an arrangement is in place, so progress in some policy areas may be made before the arrangement goes into effect.

If IMF staff and officials decide that enough overall progress has been made, the loan is disbursed. If not, the loan is suspended or the agreement is cancelled. In some cases, when it is obvious that policy targets have not been achieved, the IMF can grant a "waiver" and continue to disburse the loan. Even if all of these decisions were completely transparent and free from international politics, which they are probably not, the ultimate decision to disburse the loan relies on IMF judgment about the progress made across the various policy conditions.

One can design an aggregate index much differently than the ones so far presented. Consider the work of researchers at the IMF, Valerie Mercer-Blackman and Anna Unigovskaya.[12] They distinguish between two types of conditions – structural benchmarks and performance criteria – creating two indices of compliance. They call the first the Structural Benchmark Index and the second the Index of Fund Program Implementation. Within each index several different types of conditions are included. The Structural Benchmark Index includes required conditions in seven different areas: trade/exchange systems, pricing and marketing, public enterprise, tax/expenditure reform, financial sector, privatization reform, and "other." The Index of Fund Program Implementation or "Quantitative Implementation Index" includes quantitative targets across many different economic policy dimensions, such as fiscal balance. Both indexes essentially indicate the number of conditions that were met (as deemed by the IMF – so the indexes rely on IMF judgment, like the measures discussed above) as a proportion of the total number of conditions that were prescribed.[13]

Consider some examples from the Mercer-Blackman and Unigovskaya data, which cover Eastern Europe from 1989 to 1997. Under one SBA, Bulgaria faced just one structural condition, falling under the "Pricing and Marketing" category. Latvia also faced only one structural condition under an SBA, but it fell under the "Tax/expenditure reform" category. In both of these cases, only partial compliance was achieved, so both countries receive a score of 50 percent on the Structural Benchmark Index. They receive the same score, but they were required to fulfill quite different policy conditions, and they each undertook different actions. As another example, Georgia and Kyrgyzstan both achieved scores of 79 on the Structural Benchmark Index under ESAF programs, but Kyrgyzstan faced 35 different structural conditions, while Georgia faced 22. Kyrgyzstan faced one condition under the "Trade/exchange systems" category, while Georgia faced none in this category. Georgia faced two conditions under the "Pricing and Marketing" category, while Kyrgyzstan faced none in this category. In other words, vastly different experiences under IMF programs are often coded as the same. One loses a lot of information about which exact policies countries complied with when one aggregates all information into just an overall index.

Note, however, that there are several encouraging features of Mercer-Blackman and Unigovskaya's data that should be highlighted. First, by breaking implementation into two categories, there is not an overall score for compliance. Instead, there are two overall scores: a score for compliance with structural conditions, and a score for performance conditions. Second, both indexes are constructed from data on the actual conditions. So, this approach verges on disaggregating compliance, by at least breaking up conditions into two indexes. These indexes in turn are constructed from further disaggregated data – the actual policy conditions for each arrangement. The Mercer-Blackman and Unigovskaya data set, which come from the IMF database for Monitoring Fund Arrangements (MONA), opens the door to the disaggregated approach to measuring compliance.

One final reason in favor of a disaggregate approach is that the aggregate indexes of IMF compliance are not very highly correlated. Consider Table 5.1, adapted from an IMF Working Paper, which reports correlation coefficients between various measures of compliance discussed above, covering arrangements from 1992–2002.[14] Generally speaking, correlation coefficients can potentially range from –1 (for measures that vary in perfectly opposite directions) to +1 (for measures that vary exactly the same); 0 indicates no correlation at all. There is no magic threshold for how highly two different measures of the same phenomenon should be, but debates rage in political science, for example, over measures of democracy that are correlated in ranges above 0.9. In Table 5.1, none of the correlation coefficients even break the threshold of 0.7. The one that comes closest is the correlation between "Programs with no irreversible interruptions" and "Percentage of the loan drawn." It is not surprising that these two measures have the highest correlation, since disbursements of IMF loans should stop

Table 5.1 Correlations between different measures of compliance

Measure of compliance	Percentage of the loan drawn	Quantitative Implementation Index	Structural Benchmark Index
Quantitative Implementation Index	0.30		
Structural Benchmark Index	0.35	0.29	
Programs with no "irreversible interruptions"	0.70	0.31	0.29

during an interruption (almost by definition). If anything, it is surprising that the correlation coefficient is so low. The correlations between the other measures of compliance are lower still, ranging from 0.35 to 0.29. At least the correlations are all in the expected direction; these measures do have a tendency to move in the same direction.

Disaggregate approaches to measuring compliance

A disaggregate approach to measuring compliance with IMF arrangements follows a different logic than the aggregate measures discussed above. Instead of looking at one simple overall measure, this approach recognizes that the determinants and consequences of compliance in different policy dimensions may not be the same. It is easier to raise interest rates than it is to reform pension systems, so rates of compliance may be different for these two types of conditions. The effects of compliance with different conditions may also be different. Raising interest rates may have an immediate negative impact on economic growth, while reforming a pension system may have a long run positive impact on economic growth. Studying the effect of an overall level of compliance may not be as useful as looking at the effects of specific policies.

Ironically, while all of the recent work on compliance uses aggregate indexes, the earliest work on compliance used disaggregated approaches. Dreher cites a 1980 study by IMF economists W. A. Beveridge and Margaret Kelly as the first to look at the question of compliance.[15] They considered compliance rates with *fiscal conditions* and *bank credit ceilings* separately, looking at 105 countries that participated in IMF Stand-By Arrangements between 1969 and 1978. They found that for cases with fiscal conditions, the compliance rate was 62 percent, and for cases with bank credit ceiling conditions, the compliance rate was 55 percent.[16] Polak expanded this study to consider further arrangements. He reports that for 34 SBA and EFF arrangements in 1983, compliance with the fiscal conditions was 36 percent, while compliance with the credit ceiling conditions was 44 percent. For 17 SAF arrangements in 1988–1989, compliance for both types of conditions was 40 percent, and for five ESAF arrangements in 1988–1989, compliance with both types of conditions was 60 percent. For all programs considered by Polak, this gives a compliance rate of 54 percent for fiscal conditions and 51 percent for bank credit ceiling conditions. The overall rates of compliance across these two conditions were not very different, but consider what was found in a different study.

Part of Polak's data come from a 1989 study by Sebastian Edwards, who looked at compliance with three different types of conditions: changes in deficit (fiscal), ceilings on domestic credit, and ceilings on net domestic credit to the government.[17] Note that the fiscal category has to do with the taxing and spending activities of the government, which, if there is a legislature, may not be completely under the control of the finance minister or the executive branch of the government. The other two categories – domestic credit and credit to the government – may, in many countries, be under the control of the executive branch, either under a finance minister or the central bank.

Edwards considered the 34 programs that were approved in 1983 and tracked compliance over three years. He found that compliance with fiscal conditions was 30 percent in 1983, 19 percent in 1984, and 44 percent in 1985. Interestingly, a new IMF Independent Evaluation Office study of 133 programs in 70 countries from 1985 to 2000 finds that 40 percent of the cases complied – indeed "overperformed" with respect to deficit targets, although 60 percent "underperformed." The average achievement was about one-half of the target fiscal balance. In the early Edwards study, compliance with the other two conditions was higher than this on average. For changes in domestic credit, compliance was 55 percent in 1983, 46 percent in 1984, and 41 percent in 1985. Compliance was highest for changes in net domestic credit to the government: 72 percent in 1983, 53 percent in 1984, and 52 percent in 1985. Thus, overall the compliance rates were: 31 percent for fiscal conditions, 47 percent for domestic credit, and 59 percent for credit to the government. Edwards emphasizes the low rate of compliance with the fiscal conditions, noting that the deficit target "in no year reached a 50 percent rate of compliance."[18]

Why is there such variance of compliance rates for different conditions? This is a question that has not yet been addressed in the literature on IMF programs. Perhaps compliance rates vary across different types of conditions because certain governments face veto players and interest groups that have more say over some policy areas than others. Recall that the Letter of Intent is sent by the executive branch to the IMF. Perhaps compliance rates are highest in policy areas where the executive branch has more power. It is also possible that the government has better control over certain areas of the economy because they are less subject to exogenous shocks.

The point is to recognize that the compliance picture becomes more nuanced when one looks at disaggregated rates. Compliance may be higher in some policy areas than in others, and looking at an aggregate index masks this. Compliance rates may be high in some countries simply because they are required to comply with only a few simple conditions. One would not want to group such cases with countries that achieved high levels of compliance across many difficult conditions.

Because there is such variance in the constellations of conditions that are found in IMF arrangements, an alternative approach to studying conditionality is to be highly focused on a narrow type of conditions. Dreher reports, for example, that the 1985 study by IMF economists Justin B. Zulu and Saleh M. Nsouli focused only on the credit ceiling condition for African countries participating in IMF programs in 1980–1981.[19] They found that about half of the countries achieved the credit ceiling target.

The best such detailed work on conditions comes from a study by Erica Gould.[20] Her approach is narrow. She looks only at one specific type of condition: "bank-friendly" conditions that required repayment of debt to private financiers. Her research question is why such conditions are imposed, and she finds that they are imposed when supplemental financing is necessary for the IMF program. Recall from Chapter 2 that Gould argues that when IMF programs require additional loans from international financiers, these actors can influence the types of conditions the IMF imposes upon countries. While Gould does not address the question of compliance directly, the implication is clear. To the extent that private financial institutions hold sway over the Fund, the IMF should enforce these bank friendly conditions by withholding loans from countries that do not comply.

Gould's work is valuable not simply because she collected actual data on conditions – although this contribution should not be understated. More importantly, rather than develop some overall index of conditionality, she collected data on a specific type of condition. She then studied why this precise condition was imposed. Her path-breaking work is a model study from which others should build.

This line of reasoning leads to a new line of research questions about compliance. First, there is a *selection* question: Why are certain conditions imposed in some cases but not others? Is conditionality driven by purely economic factors or do political factors – both international and domestic – play a role? Second, there is a *performance* question: Which countries comply with which types of conditions? Is compliance uniformly high across certain policy areas and low across others? Or does compliance with specific conditions depend on the type of country – whether it is a democracy or not, the number of veto players, the fractionalization of the country? Finally, this kind of approach leads to a whole new way to evaluate IMF program effectiveness. Instead of asking what the overall (or aggregate) effect of IMF programs is, one asks what the effects of specific policies under IMF programs have been.

As Polak suggested for future work in his 1991 essay: "it might be better to leave the general question [of overall program effectiveness] unanswered and to concentrate instead on analyzing the effects of Fund-type *policies*" (emphasis in the original).[21] Along these lines, Axel Dreher and Roland Vaubel have researched how the *number of conditions* included in an IMF arrangement impact key policy targets, such as fiscal and monetary targets. They find no correlation – which they take as evidence of low levels of compliance.[22]

Yet, these types of questions can be better addressed with a disaggregated approach to studying compliance. For example, how, specifically, do different types of fiscal conditions impact actual fiscal policies? Specific questions of this sort have not yet been addressed in the literature on IMF programs. New research, however, does address the determinants of overall levels of compliance, as the next section reviews.

The determinants of compliance

Regardless of how one measures it, there is great variance in the rates at which countries comply with IMF agreements. Why do some countries comply and others do not? As research on this question is new, the results should be interpreted with caution – the findings are tentative. Nonetheless, the results are plausible and promising.

A 2003 study by IMF economists Anna Ivanova, Alexandros Mourmouras, and George Anayiotas along with Professor Wolfgang Mayer of the University of Cincinnati analyzes three different measures of compliance: non-interruption of programs, percentage of loan disbursed, and an overall index of implementation (constructed from the quantitative implementation index and the structural benchmark index).[23] They look for factors that tended to have effects across these various indicators of compliance, considering a data set of 170 SBA, EFF, and ESAF programs approved between 1992 and 1998.

They find that several domestic political factors influence compliance. They summarize their results as follows: the presence of strong special interests in the legislature – measured by the largest percentage of legislative seats controlled by a party representing nationalistic, religious, rural, and regional interest groups – makes compliance less likely. In contrast, countries with a high degree of political cohesion – as measured by the similarity of the political parties controlling the executive and the legislature – are more likely to comply. Countries facing political instability are less likely to comply, although they find that if there is an effective bureaucracy in place, political turnover plays less of a role.

IMF economists Saleh M. Nsouli, Rouben Atoian, and Alexandros Mourmouras expand upon the study above analyzing a larger set of data (197 programs from the 1992–2002 period).[24] They focus on two measures of compliance: loan disbursement, and irreversible interruptions. Their work shows that there are practically no factors that predict both of these measures of compliance with any great degree of statistical significance.

Indeed, there is just one such factor, "internal conflict," a measure of political violence. Strangely, lower levels of political violence lead to lower disbursements of the loan and greater chance of an irreversible interruption. The authors believe this is because the IMF is often involved in countries where "observance of the law is not very good."[25] Apparently, the IMF practices lenience with such countries – the authors state the finding as:

> more IMF financing is disbursed and fewer interruptions are experienced in countries in which internal conflict was intense and law enforcement weak before program approval. Arguably, this reflects the IMF's role, as lender and policy adviser, in facilitating the return to normalcy of countries experiencing natural or political shocks.[26]

As for the rest of the factors the authors examine, none has a statistically significant impact on both measures of compliance.

None of the economic factors they examine – GDP per capita, inflation, fiscal deficit, current account, investment profile rating, size of IMF quota, or economic growth – influence loan disbursements. The same is true for irreversible interruptions, except for economic growth, which has a slightly significant impact – higher economic growth makes an irreversible interruption less likely.

Many political variables[27] are also not significant: quality of bureaucracy, democratic accountability, external conflict, religious tensions, and socioeconomic conditions rating. Other variables matter for one measure of compliance but not the other. So, for example, lower ethnic tensions lead to greater loan disbursements, but have no effect on irreversible interruptions. The same is true for greater government stability.

Dreher echoes this pattern: "With respect to the compliance indices ... results are somewhat disappointing. No clear pattern emerges as to what factors are important for compliance."[28] Yet, one factor that Dreher, as well as Joseph Joyce, economist of Wellesley College, cite as important is *democracy*.[29] Democracies appear to be more likely to comply than dictatorships in these studies. Joyce points out, however, that when the government of a democracy faces a high degree of partisan polarization, compliance is less likely. The index of polarization that Joyce uses takes on a value of 0 if the political party of the president or prime minister enjoys a majority in the legislature, and 1 or 2 if opposition parties control the legislature (1 if the ideological difference is small, 2 if not – an admittedly subjective judgment). It turns out that according to Joyce's estimations, the polarization effect trumps the effect of democracy, so that a highly polarized democracy is less likely to comply with an IMF program than a dictatorship.

Perhaps with better measures of compliance more will be learned. For now, one can conclude that both international and domestic politics influence compliance. Countries important to the IMF major shareholders face less pressure to comply, and countries with greater institutionalized opposition face greater obstacles to comply.

Note that behind all of these conclusions, however, lurks another "selection problem": Which countries get which conditions? Do all countries facing the same economic circumstances receive the same level of conditionality or does the IMF account for international and domestic political factors when designing an IMF program? Recall from Chapter 2 that international political factors may influence the level of conditionality a country receives – Dreher and Jensen find that allies of the US are more likely to receive fewer conditions than other countries; Dreher, Sturm, and I find that countries serving as a rotating members of the UN Security Council also receive fewer conditions.[30]

Or take the democracy finding, for example, that democracies are more likely to comply than dictatorships. Perhaps the IMF recognizes that democracies face veto players that dictatorships do not, and thus grants them softer conditions. This may account for the higher rates of compliance among democracies, rather than an inherent propensity of democracies to keep their international commitments. If democracies do not get softer treatment, however, then the higher rates of compliance may be an indicator that democracies indeed make more credible commitments than dictatorships. Answers to such "selection" questions with respect to compliance await more detailed information on IMF arrangements.

The effects of compliance

This chapter began by explaining that in order to answer the question of the effectiveness of the IMF one must first answer the question of compliance. By now it should be clear that the question of what drives compliance has not yet been adequately researched. The question of how to measure compliance is not straightforward, and there is still more work to be done. Thus, the chapter will not be able to settle the debate about whether IMF programs have their effects via compliance with policies or via loans. Nevertheless, it is worth presenting the evidence that does exist since it has dealt with data and measurement problems in various clever ways.

First consider the evidence presented in the extensive study by Nsouli, Atoian, and Mourmouras, presented in the previous section. They present evidence about the effect of compliance on inflation and growth.

Regarding economic growth, they find that compliance has no effect! Recall that Nsouli and colleagues consider two measures of compliance: percentage of the loan drawn and irreversible interruptions. They find that receiving higher percentages of the loan does not help growth, and receiving IMF punishment by being cut off from loans does not hurt growth. This suggests that the negative effects IMF programs have had on growth come through policies not the IMF loan – otherwise, higher rates of compliance would lead to better results.

Dreher's research on compliance (cited above) produces even stronger findings on growth. He finds that the overall effect of IMF programs on economic growth is negative. Compliance with IMF programs tends to mitigate this negative effect – but not enough. Even for countries that comply, the impact of IMF programs on economic growth is negative. The effect of the size of an IMF loan as a percentage of GDP has no impact on growth.[31] The Michael Hutchison and Ilan Noy study finds the same: IMF programs hurt growth even after controlling for levels of compliance.

Recalling the left-right debate on IMF programs, these growth results are not conclusive for either side, but it tends to favor the left:

loans do not appear to have a negative effect on growth, so IMF programs do not appear to be subsidizing bad policy. And compliance with IMF programs does not result in a positive effect on growth either. Even when countries comply with IMF programs at high levels, there is no evidence of a positive effect on economic growth.

What about inflation? Recall Stone's study of Eastern Europe. He recognizes that the effect of IMF policy conditions depends on whether countries actually comply with the policies, but also that compliance is not straightforward to measure. Yet, Stone has evidence that some countries are more likely to be punished for noncompliance than others. In particular, countries that do not enjoy preferential treatment from the United States are likely to be severely punished for noncompliance, while countries that are important to the US are not likely to face serious punishment. So Stone incorporates the credibility of punishment into his evaluation of the effectiveness of IMF programs on inflation. He finds that for countries preferred by the US – where the credibility of punishment is low – IMF programs do not improve inflation. And where the credibility of punishment is high – in countries that are not favored by the US – IMF programs are actually effective against inflation. IMF programs lower inflation in countries where IMF conditionality is enforced. Economists at the IMF, Nsouli, Atoian, and Mourmouras, also find some evidence that compliance with IMF programs does lead to lower rates of inflation.[32]

This is evidence in favor of the critics of the IMF from the right. Often IMF programs are not enforced, and when they are not enforced they are not effective. When they are enforced, however, the policies have shown success at curtailing inflation. Unfortunately, the same cannot be said for growth.

Conclusion

Measuring compliance with IMF programs is not straightforward, and it is no accident that many studies of the effects of IMF programs, reviewed in Chapter 4, have avoided this issue. Yet, the question of compliance is too important to be ignored. To address important debates about how the IMF should be reformed, one needs a thorough understanding about what determines compliance and what are the effects. The studies reviewed in this chapter have taken important steps forward in addressing the compliance question. We know that compliance is far from 100 percent, and that compliance rates differ across different policy areas. Compliance has been cited as being as high as 72 percent for credit creation conditions and as low as 30 percent for fiscal conditions. We also know that economic factors do not completely explain why some countries comply and others do not. Instead, international and domestic political factors appear to play roles in determining who complies. As for the effects of compliance, there is evidence that the effect of IMF programs on inflation depends on the extent of compliance, although rates of economic growth appear to be negative regardless of compliance levels.

What do we still need to know? To be blunt, we need to know a lot more. Compliance is a ripe research topic on the IMF. In general, we need to know *why* some countries comply and some do not. More specifically, we need to know why some countries comply with *specific conditions* and some do not.

Once we have a handle on the questions of who complies with which policies and why they choose to do so, there will be a solid foundation upon which to answer perhaps the most important questions: What are the effects of complying with certain specific IMF policy conditions?

As one might imagine, since there is little agreement on the answers to the questions laid out in this chapter, debates rage about how to improve the IMF. The debate about the reform of the IMF is the subject of the next chapter.

6 Reform the IMF?

In 1997, following decades of economic growth, crisis struck the economies of Thailand, Indonesia, South Korea, the Philippines, Hong Kong, and Malaysia. Up to this point, these economies had been lauded by the IMF as part of an "East Asian miracle" of economic development. By 1998, the effects of the East Asian financial crisis were felt as far away as Russia, Brazil, and even the United States. In 2001, Argentina, a country considered to be a "model student" of the IMF throughout the 1990s, entered into a severe financial crisis. The IMF was implicated by many as playing a role in exacerbating these crises, and – for the first time in the history of the institution – calls for its reform and even its dissolution came from across the political spectrum.[1]

The debate has largely focused on the question of whether the IMF should be in the "development business." Although national prosperity, full employment and increasing real incomes were among the IMF original goals, both John Maynard Keynes and Harry Dexter White saw a division of labor between the IMF and the World Bank. As described by political economist Richard Feinberg of the University of California at San Diego, White called for the IMF to concentrate on disruptions of foreign exchange, leaving the Bank economic recovery; Keynes called for the IMF to be staffed with "cautious bankers" and the Bank with "imaginative expansionists." Yet, the distinction between the two institutions tasks was not obvious, and had to be clarified in a 1966 memorandum, assigning to the IMF the primary responsibility of *temporary* stabilization assistance.[2] Recall from Chapter 1 that the first IMF arrangement with a developing country in 1954 was not even temporary – it lasted four years. And distinctions between the IMF and the World Bank became blurred further in the 1970s and 1980s when the IMF opened lending facilities officially designed to last up to four years. The IMF was never able to restrict itself to the founding fathers' ideal of temporary lending. Many people, however, pose the question: Should this international institution be involved in promoting economic development? Or should the role of policy conditionality be reduced – scaled back to the more moderate levels originally envisaged by the founders of the institution?

On the one hand, if the IMF is to remain in the business of promoting economic development, how should it proceed? Why is there a dearth of evidence of success? What has gone wrong and what needs to change? On the other hand, if the IMF is to scale back its operations, what should the role of conditionality be? Should there even be conditionality, and if not, how can the Fund address the question of moral hazard?

This chapter reviews various prominent positions that have been taken on the question of economic reform, as well as discuss the directions that the IMF in fact has taken to change its ways. Disagreement exists at almost every level: What causes economic crises? What has the IMF done? Why has it failed?

The basic disagreement follows the compliance debate from the previous chapter: people from the left tend to criticize the policies imposed through IMF conditionality. People from the right tend to criticize the loans provided by the IMF. One side assumes compliance with incorrect policy conditions hurts countries, while the other side assumes noncompliance and believes that IMF loans subsidize the incorrect policies that were in place in recipient countries to begin with.

Despite disagreement on these questions, there exists a strange consensus among the IMF's critics from the left and the right about how the IMF should be reformed. They agree that a major problem has been a lack of *transparency*, and they argue that the operations of the IMF should be *scaled back*.

There is also consensus that a major hurdle faced by the IMF is the domestic politics within program countries. This hurdle appears too high to most, which is one of the reasons people feel IMF operations should be reduced.

Yet, the IMF does not see domestic politics as insurmountable. So, while the number of new economic programs the IMF initiates each year has dropped moderately in the new century, the depth of these programs with respect to domestic politics has increased.

The major innovations the IMF has introduced since the East Asian financial crisis are increased *transparency* and country *ownership* of their economic programs. Before looking into these IMF reforms, however, consider the critiques from the left and the right in greater detail.[3]

Critique from the left

Nobel Prize laureate Joseph Stiglitz, who served as the Chairman of the Council of Economic Advisors under President Bill Clinton (1995–1997) and served as the chief economist and senior vice president at the World Bank (1997–2000), offers a scathing and thorough critique of the IMF in his book, *Globalization and Its Discontents*.[4] He cites the major problem as being the policies the IMF imposes, and he traces the roots of this problem back to the very incentives that IMF staff and officials respond to – notably, that they act on behalf of foreign investors and domestic elites at the expense of labor and the poor in program countries.[5]

The irony for Stiglitz is that while the IMF was founded because markets fail, the policies imposed by the Fund provide little role for non-market solutions. The advice of the IMF assumes that markets, if left to their own devices, will correct all problems in the long run. Yet, the IMF is itself a non-market solution to a market failure. The IMF exists because markets fail, and yet its economists espouse utter confidence in markets. Stiglitz thus finds the Fund to be "plagued with intellectual inconsistencies."[6]

Recall from Chapter 1 that one of the founding fathers of the IMF, John Maynard Keynes, noted that economic downturns in one country imposed negative externalities on other countries, and that markets did not address this adequately. By pooling resources under an organization like the IMF, funds could be lent to countries facing economic crisis to maintain global levels of employment and consumption so that economic problems would not spill over needlessly from country to country. The IMF was invented to cope with failures of markets.

Yet, the IMF seeks to reduce the role of governments in markets through fiscal austerity, privatization of national assets, and market liberalization from government regulation. Economists at the IMF assume that markets will quickly arise in the absence of government action, thus the role of government is required to be diminished. Stiglitz argues, however, that some government actions are in place precisely because markets fail to provide an essential service, and are doomed to fail again because of missing insurance markets or limited information. Stiglitz further claims that sometimes the recipe prescribed by the IMF is not well thought out because the interaction of various policies can be detrimental to the economy: trade liberalization with high interest rates leads to unemployment and job destruction; liberalization of financial markets without safeguard regulations can lead to economic volatility; privatization without ensuring competition can lead to higher prices for consumers; fiscal austerity under an economic crisis can increase unemployment and deepen the crisis.[7]

Stiglitz notes that advanced industrialized countries do not follow austerity policies themselves when they face economic downturns. He points out, for example, that when the United States faced a recession in 2001, "the debate was not whether there should be a stimulus package, but its design."[8] Contractionary policies, such as those suggested by the IMF, were certainly not considered by the US government. Stiglitz thinks that similar stimulus packages could serve to help developing countries grow their way out of economic crises. Renewed economic growth also would reassure investors, which would further reinforce a positive trajectory for the economy.

So Stiglitz questions why the IMF pursues the policies that it does, especially in the face of evidence that the policies have failed to promote long run economic growth in the developing world. He reasons that the IMF is not just concerned with maintaining global stability, but is "also pursuing the interests of the financial community."[9] It is important to note that Stiglitz only hints at possible mechanisms by which the IMF has incentives to pursue the interests of global financiers. He suggests that there is a revolving door between the financial community and positions at the IMF, but he does not provide any examples of people moving from one position to another. Erica Gould, on the other hand, provides a mechanism by which the IMF may be beholden to private financiers. As described in Chapter 2, she finds that the IMF often relies on the financial community for supplemental financing for its programs and that the Fund repays private financiers by imposing bank-friendly conditions on program countries.

With such connections between the financial community and the IMF in mind, Stiglitz paints an insidious picture of the Fund: when a developing country faces a balance of payments crisis, the IMF extends loans of foreign exchange so that the currency does not have to be immediately devalued. This buys time for foreign financiers and the domestic elite to exchange the collapsing currency for a stable currency at favorable terms. These actors can get their money out of the country through the liberalized markets which the IMF has imposed upon the country. After this, the currency is finally devalued, and labor and the poor are left with the debt of repaying the IMF loan with a devalued currency. The evidence on income distribution and IMF programs supports this point of view.

What should be done to reform the IMF according to this view? The crucial change that is necessary according to Stiglitz is a change in the policies the IMF imposes as part of conditionality.

First, he stresses the dangers of capital market liberalization. By instead imposing short term capital controls and exit taxes, governments can make it more costly for foreigners and domestic elites to pull their resources out of a country in crisis, discouraging the crisis from deepening.

Stiglitz also argues that the IMF should rely less on lending to countries in crisis and instead focus on managing bankruptcy. Such an approach would be less costly to labor and the poor, and would place responsibility for the crisis on actors who should have been wary of the risks of over-investing in the first place.

Finally, with respect to lending, the IMF should return to the mandate proposed by Keynes: "providing funds to restore aggregate demand in countries facing an economic recession."[10] Stiglitz argues that the best way out of an economic crisis is to restore confidence through policies that maintain employment and consumption, not through the contractionary policies the IMF has relied on. To the extent that costly economic adjustments must be made, Stiglitz favors transparency about these costs – as part of the arrangement the IMF should disclose the expected impact on poverty and unemployment.

How can such changes take effect? Stiglitz suggests two main reforms to achieve the above changes: transparency and governance. *Transparency* is an issue that nearly everyone raises. The IMF was too secretive in the past, and there can be little accountability without information on the actions and policies of the IMF. The lack of transparency is one of the reasons that Stiglitz's contentions about the insidious nature of the Fund are plausible to many. People may come to all sorts of conclusions about important negotiations that routinely take place behind closed doors. Most suggest that transparency will make the IMF more accountable, and that transparency will help settle debates about the level of policy conditionality the Fund imposes and levels of noncompliance. Yet, Stiglitz believes that transparency has the potential to do even more. He believes that with transparency there can be open debates over the policies of the IMF. In other words, Stiglitz is hopeful that transparency will not just reveal IMF policy prescriptions but even transform IMF policy prescriptions.

Stiglitz also places a lot of faith in changing the *governance* of the IMF: "the most fundamental change that is required to make globalization work in the way it should is a change in governance."[11] Presently, the governance of the IMF favors countries that do not participate in IMF programs. Ten of the 24 seats on the Executive Board are filled by Europeans – an eleventh is held by the US. This leaves just five for Asia, three for Latin America, three for the Middle East and North

> **To the reader**
>
> How many of the current Executive Directors come from countries that have participated in recent IMF arrangements? Check who currently sits on the Executive Board by looking up "IMF Executive Directors and Voting Power" on the IMF website. Then check recent IMF Annual Reports to see if any come from countries that have participated in recent IMF programs.

Africa, and just two for Africa south of the Sahara. Of the 24 people who presently sit on the Executive Board, only six of them come from countries that have actually participated in IMF programs in the past ten years. Yet, Ngaire Woods, the Director of the Global Economic Governance Programme at University College Oxford, points out the following: with the exception of only the US, all of the original major shareholders at the IMF were expected to be recipient countries.[12]

To change the governance of the IMF, Stiglitz argues that first the size of the Executive Board should be expanded so that there are more seats at the table for African countries as well as other recipient countries. Even if official vote shares are not altered, the fact of having more recipient country voices around the table may open debates about what policies should be attached to IMF loans. This suggestion is consistent with the spirit of Executive Board meetings, considering that votes are rarely taken on the Board, and that the IMF operates according to the "consensus" of meetings.

In addition, Stiglitz believes that the actual distribution of votes at the IMF should change. He is not alone – even the current Managing Director of the Fund, Rodrigo de Rato, supports the idea.[13] Ariel Buira, Director of the G-24 Secretariat and former IMF staff member and Executive Director, has proposed a formula by which governance at the IMF can be recalibrated.[14] Recall from Chapter 1 that vote share at the IMF is determined by a country's economic size and exposure to trade. These economic variables can be measured in various manners. GDP, for example, can be calibrated using exchange rates, although this practice tends to understate the GDP of developing countries, where valuable non-tradable services are undercounted because the cost of labor is less expensive – a haircut may be worth the same to people in different countries, but it may cost as much as 50 times more in New York than in the Dominican Republic according to official exchange rates. For this reason, almost all cross-national research in political science and economics – and, in particular, almost all cross-national work *at the IMF* – uses GDP measured in terms of purchasing power parity (PPP). Yet when calculating subscriptions to the IMF, the IMF uses GDP measured in terms of exchange rates. Why does the IMF use market rate GDP? The standard argument is that this best reflects a country's ability to contribute to IMF efforts to finance balance of payments problems. But Buira points out that contributions to the IMF amount to less than one percent of GDP, so the "ability to pay" argument is not persuasive. Developing countries could contribute more to the IMF; this would give them a stronger voice.

Indeed, if the IMF were to switch to using GDP measured in terms of PPP, the voting shares of many countries would dramatically change. The major shareholder's votes would not change very much – the US would still have the most voting power by far. But smaller industrialized countries, like Belgium or Denmark, would have their vote shares cut a great deal. The windfall would go to emerging market countries. China, for example, would have nearly double the votes of Japan – instead of the other way around, which is the way it is currently. Belgium would have less than one third of the votes that Brazil would have – presently Belgium has 50 percent more votes than Brazil.

One question behind reforming the governance of the IMF, however, looms large: What difference would it make? One can easily justify why voting shares should change, but in terms of reforming the IMF, would a new distribution of votes change the way the IMF operates? The Stiglitz critique calls for the IMF to pursue different policies during economic crises, but it is not obvious that new policies would follow from governance reform.

One innovation might be the creation of a new "rapid insurance" facility to rush loans to strong economies if hit by a serious shock.[15] As governance stands, the powerful members of the Fund fear the perverse incentives of moral hazard that this facility could induce. A new facility like this might go into effect, however, if governance changed at the IMF because the idea is supported by large emerging market countries, like Brazil, for example. The goal of this reform would be to stop financial contagion.

This kind of reform is consistent with suggestions of the late Yale University economist, James Tobin. Recognizing that increasing integration of markets and world trade is likely to increase the volatility of a country's balance of payments, Tobin suggests that the IMF increase the quotas of member countries so that greater amounts of foreign exchange are available to assist countries in times of crisis. This would raise the amount of money a country can take within the 25 percent cutoff – without submitting to IMF conditionality.[16]

So changing governance could have some effects. But as for conditionality under IMF programs, would changes in governance generate changes in policy? There are at least four reasons to question whether governance reform would make much of a difference with respect to policy conditionality under IMF programs.

First of all, even with governance reform, the United States would still have the most votes. Unless reform were extreme, the US would retain veto power over major decisions. To paraphrase a recent conversation I had with former Brazilian and Mexican government officials, increasing Brazilian and Mexican voting power at the IMF would certainly be the correct thing to do, but it would not be consequential – the United States would still call the tune at the IMF.

Second, to the extent the IMF is beholden to private financiers, vote share at the IMF would not matter. Private financiers would not change their demands, and if IMF programs require their financial support, their preferred "bank friendly" conditions would still be necessary to include in IMF programs.

Third, it is not obvious that increased representation from the developing world would change the actual voting over IMF policies. Perhaps a stronger voice for China – a country that has succeeded economically following policies quite different from those espoused by the Fund – would make a difference. But China is unique among the membership of the IMF. To the extent that elites from finance ministries and central banks around the world share similar world views with Western powers, a change in vote shares might not make much difference. This may be especially true if the management and staff also come from the same educational background, as Bessma Momani has shown.[17]

Stiglitz himself has pointed out that part of the problem with the implementation of IMF programs has been the actions of elites in program countries:

> There is ... a process of self-selection of reforms: the ruling elite has taken advantage of the reform process and the asymmetries of information – both between themselves and the citizenry and between the international aid community and themselves – to push those reforms that would benefit them.[18]

More representation for the developing world does not necessarily imply more representation for labor and the poor of the developing world.

The fourth problem with governance reform is that even extreme governance reform will not make the IMF a democratically accountable institution. Ngaire Woods stresses that governance reform should be pursued, but also warns that it is no panacea for the problems of accountability that plague the IMF. Recall the long chain of command that was laid out in Chapter 2 – the actions of the IMF staff are simply too far removed from the Executive Board, which in turn is too far removed from the Board of Governors, which in turn is too far removed from the direct control of the citizens of the world they supposedly represent. As pointed out by Robert Dahl, one of the most important political scientists of the twentieth century, international organizations simply lack the capacity to be as accountable as domestic political systems because they are not subject to the major mechanism that citizens have to hold their officials accountable: elections.[19]

In fact, better representation for the developing world at the IMF might even make the IMF less accountable. Recall from Chapter 2 the argument of Roland Vaubel that spreading the control of the IMF over more countries reduces the incentive of any one country to exert the effort of overseeing the international bureaucracy. Diluting control also dilutes monitoring incentives.[20]

Woods and Dahl suggest that ultimately we should be wary of ceding too much authority to the IMF.[21] Stiglitz also agrees that while it would be best to have the IMF pursue different policies than it has in the past, it should also become less involved in the domestic politics of program countries. He suggests that the IMF narrow its focus, moving away from development and towards data collection and the surveillance of economies. Not only is such data collection important for bringing about higher global levels of transparency, but narrowing the focus of the Fund also engenders greater accountability.

Critique from the right

Interestingly, scaling back the operations of the IMF is similarly suggested by moderate and conservative critics of the IMF. They also agree that the Fund should be more transparent and focus more on data collection and surveillance rather than on promoting economic development. Conservative economists also agree with Stiglitz that the IMF should rely less on lending and more on bankruptcy so that actors who are tempted to over invest in a country face potential costs for their actions.

The agreement that exists at far ends of the political spectrum is surprising, and it is all the more so because people have reached these similar conclusions for different reasons. Critics from the left blame IMF *policies* for failure, implicitly assuming that governments have actually followed IMF advice. More moderate and conservative critics, however, cite low levels of *compliance* with IMF policy prescriptions.

They blame international politics for the IMF's failure to enforce conditionality. They also blame the domestic politics of recipient countries for not complying with sound advice.

The thinking about domestic politics has become more sophisticated since the early days of the IMF.[22] Early theories described balance of payments crises as the result of government deficits. If governments finance deficits by printing money, this leads to inflation, prompting people to exchange the inflationary money for more stable foreign currency, causing the government's foreign reserves to drop. The role of the IMF in this situation is clear: provide a loan to shore up the government's foreign reserves and put a stop to inflation, but also reduce the domestic supply of money by imposing fiscal and monetary austerity, through conditionality.

Eichengreen points out that such theories treat governments as naïve – even foolish.[23] Governments can take actions without IMF help. For example, perceiving a balance of payments crisis, governments can borrow from abroad to replenish reserves. They can raise interest rates. They can defend the currency on their own *if they choose*. The problem, however, may be that the domestic political costs may be too high. Higher interest rates may have unacceptable political costs in the short run: (1) high levels of unemployment, (2) domestic defaults on loans, which can hurt a weak banking system, and (3) an overextended government if there is too much short term debt. The choice to defend the currency thus depends on prospects for economic growth, the strength of the banking system, and the "political will" of the government. The IMF can play a role here by providing a loan to soften the blow of economic austerity as well as providing policy conditionality to help push through necessary economic reforms. Yet, in this situation, compliance with IMF austerity may be problematic even if governments agree with economic austerity policies and have IMF leverage to help push through some changes. There may be limits to what is politically possible.

Moreover, not all governments are so well-intentioned. Governments whose development strategies rely on domestic banks become dependent on these banks and cannot afford to let them fail. Recognizing this implicit guarantee, foreign investors rush in. When deciding how much financing to provide, investors weigh the possible return of an investment against the possibility of a loss. In a situation where the government cannot afford to let banks fail, however, foreign investors' risk of loss is reduced and overinvestment may occur. This can lead to a dangerous situation of too much short term debt. In such a situation, even a minor problem can trigger a major run on the national currency.

This is cited as one cause of the East Asian financial crisis: a kind of moral hazard on the part of *investors*, whose risks are implicitly insured by governments because they are dependent on the domestic banking system.

The role of the IMF in dealing with this kind of moral hazard is not at all clear. A proactive IMF might use "preconditionality" to impose capital controls so that the accumulation of investment is managed more carefully, both going in and coming out of countries. This runs counter, however, to the liberalization strategies the IMF tends to espouse. Others prefer a market solution – the IMF should do nothing and just let the economies fail. This will send a signal that investments really are risky, and the discipline of markets will regulate investor actions. They argue that even IMF successes have exacerbated moral hazard for investors. For example, while most people hail the successful Mexican bailout of the 1990s, when the IMF assisted in providing 50 billion dollars in loans to shore up the peso, it may have sent a signal to investors that they would be bailed out of similar situations, thereby increasing the moral hazard that led to the East Asian situation later in the decade.

According to these views, the IMF has not just failed to enforce conditionality – imposing conditionality may simply be impossible in countries that lack the "political will" to bring about economic reform. Governments dependent on the banking system simply use the IMF to bail out foreign investors. This has led many to argue that the IMF should stop acting like a "fireman" and act more like a "policeman,"[24] providing loans only to countries that follow preset conditions. Such "preconditionality" can help sort out good governments from bad.

This was one of the conclusions reached by International Financial Institutions Advisory Commission, commissioned by the US Congress in the aftermath of the East Asian crisis. This group, which came to be known as the Meltzer Commission, because it was chaired by Allan H. Meltzer, Professor of Political Economy at Carnegie Mellon University, included 11 men (six men chosen by Republicans and five men chosen by Democrats).[25]

The Meltzer Commission sees the longevity of IMF programs as evidence of their failure. Their report notes that the protracted loans of the IMF delay necessary reforms and keep governments from correcting their own mistakes. Essentially, IMF loans subsidize bad policies – the IMF continuously bails out bad governments. Thus, the Commission calls for a new mechanism "to promote steady implementation rather than superficial change. [The IMF] must create incentives to sustain reform programs until reforms have become established."

Rather than attach conditions to loans during a crisis, the Meltzer Commission advises the IMF to set up preset standards. If countries adhere to these basic standards, they should be eligible for IMF funding should a shock hit their economy. If they do not adhere to the standards, however, no loans should be provided: "Except in unusual circumstances, where the crisis poses a threat to the global economy, loans would be made only to countries in crisis that have met pre-conditions that establish financial soundness." The details of development strategies would be left to individual governments, although the IMF would certainly provide advice. The pre-conditions themselves would not contain detailed economic plans but instead be broad:

1 Countries must institute banking regulations that require adequate capitalization.
2 Countries must phase in the freedom of entry and operation for foreign financial institutions.
3 Countries borrowing from the IMF must publish the maturity structure of their outstanding sovereign and guaranteed debt and other liabilities.
4 Countries must meet a proper fiscal requirement to assure that IMF resources would not be used to sustain irresponsible budget policies.

The first pre-condition, regarding bank regulation and adequate capitalization, follows directly from the problems associated with the East Asian financial crisis. This notion receives widespread support. The second pre-condition follows – the idea here is that if countries open up to foreign financial institutions, the domestic banking system will face greater competition and become more efficient.

The third pre-condition follows the transparency fad. It requires a government to provide information on the structure of its debt, presumably so that creditors and investors would have a better notion of the risks involved with a country.

Finally, the fourth pre-condition is consistent with the traditional IMF approach to economic problems, except that now fiscal responsibility would be required before a country could gain access to IMF loans.

It might seem that preconditionality would solve the compliance problem. The incentives under preconditionality are clear: governments in compliance with the basic standards are assured of loans in the event of an emergency; governments not in compliance risk going crises alone. Yet, preconditionality introduces a credibility problem for the IMF: What if a country that is strategically or economically important to the US faces an economic crisis, but is not following preconditionality? The Meltzer Commission report itself allows for exceptions for "unusual circumstances, where the crisis poses a threat to the global economy." Presumably, preconditionality would not be enforced for countries deemed too important to let fail. Yet, according to the research presented in Chapter 2, these are precisely the problem countries. The IMF does not appear to have difficulty imposing policy conditions on unimportant countries. But countries important to the US are provided loans with conditions that are loosely enforced. It is therefore not obvious how preconditionality would solve the compliance problem as it currently exists.

Aware of this problem, the commission ultimately suggests that the role of the IMF should simply be reduced. The crucial reform suggestion of the Meltzer Commission is that "the International Monetary Fund should restrict its lending to the provision of short term liquidity. The current practice of extending long term loans for poverty reduction and other purposes should end." Furthermore, the short term loans should be offered at a penalty rate, to discourage moral hazard and to encourage prompt repayment.

The degree of agreement that the IMF should get out of the development business is remarkable. The Council on Foreign Relations, commissioned by President Clinton at the same time as the Meltzer Commission, does not advocate doing away entirely with ex-post policy conditions, but recommends that the IMF avoid long term reform programs and focus on short term crisis management.

Thomas Willett, who takes a distinctly moderate view of IMF reform, argues that the basic approach of the IMF to countries does not need fixing – the problem has been compliance. If compliance can be improved, IMF results will also improve. Willett sees compliance as a problem of international politics pressuring the IMF not to enforce conditionality for US favored countries, and also an accountability problem, which exists in all bureaucracies. The solution to the compliance problem is thus simply transparency, which will limit the influence of international politics and bring about more accountability. Yet even moderates like Willett agree that the IMF should say no more often when requests for loans are made.[26]

Hence, from across the political spectrum – left, moderate, and right – critics agree that the IMF should become a more open and transparent institution, and that it should scale back its lending operations to short term crisis lending.

The IMF response: transparency and ownership

In the aftermath of the East Asian financial crisis, the IMF undertook change. Not surprisingly, the institution did not agree with the idea of scaling back its operations, nor did it agree with critics on the left that the basic IMF approach to economic problems is incorrect.[27] The IMF did agree with critics on the right that compliance with conditionality was a problem. Better implementation would lead to better results. There was no IMF acknowledgement that US dominance of the institution is a cause of the compliance problem, but the domestic politics of recipient countries were acknowledged as a major problem. With this in mind, the two main solutions the IMF has pursued to encourage governments to comply with IMF programs are greater *transparency*, and the *ownership* of IMF economic programs by recipient country governments. Consider these changes in turn:

The first move the IMF made regarding *transparency* targeted IMF members. In 1999, the IMF adopted its *Code of Good Practices on Transparency in Monetary and Financial Policies* to make the operations of its members publicly available. With the IMF collecting and providing better information on members' monetary and financial policies, potential investors and creditors would be better able to assess country risks.

Yet, this was only part of the problem. Even with good country-level information, countries might experience dangerous levels of capital inflows if investors assume that the country will be bailed out of any financial crisis. What would the IMF do? What were the precise conditions that the IMF imposed on countries? Would conditionality be enforced? If so, which conditions and to what extent? Would some countries face stricter conditionality than others? Would some countries be bailed out no matter what? Ironically, what lacked transparency at this point was the decision-making process at the IMF itself. The IMF had imposed transparency on its members, but continued to operate in obscurity.

Many of the above questions remain unanswered, as the previous chapter revealed. The IMF took a step in the right direction, however, in January 2001, when the Executive Board took the "Transparency Decision," making information about the IMF's own operations more accessible to the public. Under this policy, the IMF publishes all country documents, provided the country gives permission. This includes publishing the annual Article IV consultations with each country as well as most Letters of Intent.

In addition, the Executive Board established in July 2001 the Independent Evaluation Office (IEO) to provide objective and independent evaluation of IMF issues. Note that this office exists outside of the regular IMF hierarchy and reports directly to the Executive Board. So, the IEO is independent of the IMF staff and management, and it even operates "at arm's length" from the Executive Board. The IEO is set up in such a way to ensure independence: the Director is appointed by the Executive Board for four-year (renewable) terms, and is prohibited from joining the IMF staff at the end of service; the Director is responsible for selecting IEO personnel, a majority of whom must come from outside the IMF. Thus, the IEO operates outside of the IMF, but can probe deeper than outsiders because it has unrestricted access to all IMF documents. It remains to be seen if this institution can clarify some of the unanswered questions raised above, but most agree that the IEO is a good idea. What it can do depends a great deal on the commitment of the Executive Board to maintain the institution's freedom to investigate and report.

There remain apparently unavoidable limits on transparency, however. Even with access to the details of IMF arrangements, the criteria for punishing noncompliance with IMF arrangements are still unclear. In contrast to the recommendations of many that the IMF should scale back conditionality to the days when IMF arrangements were at most a few pages long, many arrangements continue to be long, detailed, and covering a wide swath of policy areas. Various detailed conditions continue to be laid out in many different policy areas from poverty reduction to growth, fiscal austerity, monetary policy, trade policy, privatization, banking regulations, tax collection, financial and banking regulations, and the list goes on. Some conditions are laid out as prior actions, others have a long time horizon, and still others are subject to waivers and exceptions. Too much information – or "noise" – transmits little more information than non-transparency. And there are also documents that still remain classified.

If the IMF is to continue the practice of conditional lending, it should further streamline policy conditionality. Most importantly, if loan disbursements are to be contingent on compliance, the criteria should be made transparent – meaning *verifiable* by outsiders – and the IMF should be consistent in its enforcement.

The other recent innovation of the IMF is called *ownership*. Mohsin Khan and Sunil Sharma of the IMF Institute explain "ownership" as follows:

> Ownership of IMF-supported programs ... is an elusive concept and is hard to define or pin down. Implicitly, it refers to a situation in which the policy content of the program is similar to what the

country itself would have chosen in the absence of IMF involvement. This is because the country shares with the IMF both the objectives of the program as well as an understanding of the appropriate economic model linking those objectives to economic policies. In such a situation, the country "owns" the program in the sense that it is committed to the spirit of the program, rather than just to complying with its letter.[28]

Why does the IMF consider ownership to be an important reform? The IMF argues that ownership should solve the problem of noncompliance, and with higher rates of compliance the IMF expects better results from its programs. How does ownership work? First of all, the IMF enters into agreements only with governments that are planning to implement the reforms the IMF requires because these are the policies the government wants to pursue. The government is also expected to be an active participant in designing the program – and this participation should include more actors beyond just the finance ministry.

The problem, of course, is that this is what was supposedly happening all along. This is why IMF arrangements are spelled out in a Letter of Intent signed by the government, not the IMF. The fact that domestic politics should be accounted for in the design of IMF programs is an idea that was floated in the 1970s. Moreover, if the economic program is exactly what the government plans to pursue, why is conditionality needed? It seems that all the IMF needs is an excellent screening process by which the IMF can tell ex ante which countries really believe in economic reform and which ones are simply paying lip service just to get an IMF loan. There is, unfortunately, no such magic screening process. If there were, presumably the IMF would have been using it long ago.

Supposing, for the sake of argument, the IMF can tell which governments are honestly committed to reform and which are not, is there any role for conditionality with ownership? Economist Allan Drazen explains that there is. Suppose a government is truly committed to a program of economic reform, but faces domestic opposition. There may be program "ownership" on the part of the government in the sense that the IMF arrangement represents the policies that the government would like to pursue, but in the absence of conditionality, the policies may be vetoed by the opposition. By bringing in the IMF, the government can change the payoffs for the opposition, as the IMF loan makes policy change more lucrative and the specter of IMF punishment makes rejecting the policy change more costly. This, again, is not new, however. Political scientists have been talking about this phenomenon as far back as the 1980s, as Chapter 3 showed.

Is there anything new about ownership? One difference is that the IMF is now reaching out to broader segments of society in the development of economic programs. A 2002 IMF report on transparency notes that "Fund missions consult more regularly with a broad group of interested parties."[29] This followed a 2001 IMF staff report that suggested the IMF could reach out to trade unions, industry representatives, local non-governmental organizations, as well as actors in the government beyond the finance ministry.[30] Generally speaking, governments appear to be more involved in the drafting of their Letters of Intent. No longer is a signature the only contribution of the government. The IMF hopes that greater communication and participation will engender higher rates of compliance.[31]

Another change that came about after the East Asian financial crisis was the renaming of the Enhanced Structural Adjustment Facility to the Poverty Reduction and Growth Facility (PRGF) in September 1999. Like the ESAF, the PRGF is open only to the poorest members of the Fund, and loans are provided at a concessional rate. The programs are framed by "country-owned" Poverty Reduction Strategy Papers (PRSPs), which detail comprehensive economic reforms and development strategies. Due to their comprehensive nature, these arrangements go deeper into domestic policies than previous IMF programs.

Studies by the IMF and the IEO confirm that PRGF programs are different than standard IMF arrangements.[32] In particular, they have allowed for higher public expenditure than other IMF programs, particularly for pro-poor spending.[33] So this was more than just a change in names. This facility is explicitly where greater ownership has been fostered. Governments have been deeply involved in planning four-year long economic programs.

Notably, the IMF has shifted its resources in the direction of PRGF arrangements. From the date of the first ESAF program in 1989 up until the facility was changed to the PRGF in 1999, there were 83 ESAF programs initiated. During this same period, there were 152 standard Stand-by Arrangements initiated. From 2000 to 2005, however, PRGF programs actually outpaced Stand-by Arrangements 61 to 52.

With a total of 120 new programs initiated from 2000 to 2005, the IMF does not appear to be scaling back much. There were fewer countries under IMF programs in 2004 than in 2001 – 49 versus 62 – but the world economy has also been performing better. And where the IMF is still involved, it appears to be more deeply involved than ever.

> **To the reader**
>
> Are PRGF programs still more common than Stand-by Arrangements? Check in the most recent IMF Annual Report in Appendix II: financial operations and transactions. The Annual Reports are available at the IMF website at www.imf.org.

What is remarkable about the PRGF is that it flies in the face of everything the US Congress-commissioned report suggested. Indeed, the ownership-direction of the IMF represents a stark departure from the consensus across the political spectrum that the IMF should scale back its activities, limit its lending to short term liquidity, and get out of the development business. On the contrary, the IMF has shifted its resources, focusing on long term programs for the explicit purpose of promoting growth and reducing poverty.

The Meltzer Commission explicitly called for the new PRGF to be closed. Yet the IMF has expanded the facility. The Meltzer Commission called for *temporary* loans to be offered at *penalty* rates. Yet, the PRGF extends *long term* loans at *concessional* rates. Most critics cited the IMF's deep involvement in development strategies as an example of "mission creep" that should be scaled back. There was widespread agreement that the IMF should be less involved in the domestic politics of loan recipient countries. Yet, the PRGF is explicitly designed to foster development by delving deeply into domestic politics – more deeply than ever before.

In these senses, "ownership" should be seen as a bold stand by the IMF that the institution can do better at development than critics believe. It requires the IMF to be more selective in choosing which governments to work with, and then requires the IMF to work closely with these governments to figure out how to make economic reforms politically possible. It is a lofty goal.

Conclusion

Conditional lending has had such a poor track record, it would not surprise many to see the IMF fail. There are several reasons that conditional lending has not brought about positive change in the developing world. Even if one were to assume – contrary to Stiglitz and many other critics – that the IMF gives appropriate policy advice, conditionality may have little use.

Drawing on lessons learned throughout this book, let us imagine four sets of countries and consider the role of conditionality in each of them:

1   There are countries favored by the US for political reasons. In these situations, conditionality has no bite because the threat of the IMF to enforce conditionality is not credible. The US prevents the IMF from enforcing conditionality. There have been no reforms of the IMF to address this reality of international politics. So conditionality has little effect in these countries (and IMF loans may cause moral hazard).

2   There are countries not favored by the US whose governments agree with the policies prescribed by the IMF and face no opposition. This is the ideal "ownership" situation. Conditionality, however, is not needed in this situation. It should not do any harm, as it represents what countries would do absent the IMF. But the Fund should not be given undue credit for what governments would have pursued on their own.

3   There are countries not favored by the US whose governments use the IMF arrangement to favor domestic elite interests. This is the situation where domestic elites select which "reforms" to implement (and which not to implement), all in the name of the IMF. Here, conditionality is abused. The leverage of the IMF is used to push through unpopular policies that protect foreigners and elites during an economic crisis. Elites are able to get their assets out of a crisis situation while labor and the poor are left to pick up the pieces – and repay the IMF debt.

4   There are countries not favored by the US whose governments agree with IMF policy conditions but face opposition. One can call this the "partial ownership" situation. Assuming IMF reform policies will benefit the economic development of these countries in the long run, conditionality can help push through reforms that are generally beneficial to society in this situation.

In situations (1) and (2), conditionality does not matter much. Whether or not IMF conditionality is a good thing depends on the frequency of situation (3) versus situation (4). How common is situation (3), where conditionality is used to protect elite interests at the expense of labor and the poor? It seems fairly common. Increasing income inequality is the single most common effect of IMF programs. How common is situation (4), where IMF programs help to push through policies that face opposition in the short run but actually have positive effects in the long run? Judging by the dearth of evidence of program success in the area of economic growth, this is probably not so common. The IMF is aware of this and is making efforts to screen better the governments it assists. Hopefully, this can make situation (4) more common than situation (3).

Perhaps, however, the IMF should go further. As Stiglitz suggests, the IMF can have the expected "poverty" and "income distribution" impacts included in Letters of Intent. The IMF made a step in this direction back in 1997, when it announced its Guidelines on Social Expenditures, under which the IMF tracks health and education spending in program countries and encourages governments to include targets for these areas in their Letters of Intent. Yet, the IMF could go further by conditioning loans on compliance with these targets. This would be a remarkable new direction for conditionality, but could meet with opposition from recipient country governments, and would be difficult to monitor and enforce.

A safer bet would be to simply have the IMF scale back its operations, lending only during times of severe crisis and providing policy advice without imposing conditions.

Hopefully, of course, the new approaches of the IMF will finally work. Hopefully, the IMF will be successful and can continue to operate as it is now, with ever-improving results. Yet, if it does not – if it fails once again – hopefully, the debates laid out here will not be forgotten. With several decades' worth of chances, reform of IMF conditionality should not continue in circles. Conditionality has grown steadily since the 1950s. The problem of the 1960s and 1970s was supposedly not enough conditionality – hence the shift from macro-conditionality to micro-conditionality. The problem of the 1980s and the 1990s was supposedly too much conditionality without enough compliance – hence the shift from micro-conditionality to ownership. Maybe the IMF finally has it just right. If not, however, perhaps it is time to give conditionality up.

So this chapter concludes by making the same recommendation that many others have made: *the IMF should scale back conditionality.* Lending should be temporary, addressing only acute crisis situations. Transparency is an uncontroversial step in the right direction. But one should not hold out too much faith that more information will dramatically change the results the IMF has had in the past. Changing IMF governance is also a laudable idea, but might not have a tremendous impact. Ultimately, there are still negotiations behind closed doors and what drives the IMF to punish and reward noncompliance and policy change is still opaque. The IMF would be most effective by providing continued consultations, publishing a wealth of accurate economic data, and lending only in the direst economic circumstances.

Conclusion

The International Monetary Fund is a powerful international institution. The sum total of all contributions to the Fund is currently over 300 billion SDR. This institution can be thought of as a kind of international credit union with over 95 percent of countries in the world as members. Each member holds currency on reserve at the Fund – the amount depending on the size and importance of the member's economy – and from this pool of resources the IMF lends to countries facing various forms of economic problems.

The IMF practices "conditionality" when it lends in the hope that its loans do not simply subsidize the bad policies that led a country to borrow from the Fund in the first place. In return for continued disbursements of IMF loans, countries must follow austere policy conditions designed to ensure debt repayment, stabilize the economy, and promote national prosperity. There is little evidence, however, of the success of IMF conditionality. While there is some evidence that balance of payments problems are curtailed, there is less evidence of success with respect to inflation. Regarding economic growth, recent evidence shows that IMF programs hurt. The single most consistent effect that IMF programs appear to have is to exacerbate income inequality.

The reasons for failure are debated. On the one hand, people who believe that states have an important role to play in promoting economic growth argue that IMF austerity policies are the problem. Instead of reducing the size of the state in the face of an economic crisis, the IMF should support government stimulus packages, like those employed in the developed world during times of economic trouble. On the other hand, people who are skeptical of non-market solutions for economic problems believe that the IMF hurts countries in the opposite manner. They agree with IMF austerity but think that the IMF fails to strictly enforce conditionality. As a result, IMF loans provide a subsidy for continued economic mismanagement by developing country governments.

Surprisingly, people of these vastly divergent points of view are in broad agreement about how to fix the IMF: the Fund should scale back its economic development operations. In the aftermath of the East Asian financial crisis, the IMF faced severe criticism from across the political spectrum – many calling for the Fund to get out of the development business. In response, the international organization undertook reform. It did not agree, however, to scale back.

As I conclude this book, the most recent issue of *The Economist* is reporting that the IMF faces a 30 percent drop in its income over the next two years because, of late, the organization has not had to engage in the crisis-lending that generates its primary source of income. With the large loans provided to countries after the East Asian crisis no longer outstanding, the IMF itself faces a shortfall. This might appear as a golden opportunity for the IMF to trim back its development business operations.

Instead, however, the IMF is seeking to strengthen its role in development, delving more deeply than ever before into the domestic politics of IMF program countries. Rather than cut back, the IMF is looking to secure new, steadier sources of income. IMF Managing Director Rodrigo de Rato announced on 18 May 2006 a team of "eminent persons" to look into new ways of generating income to finance IMF activities.[1] The Public Choice view of this international bureaucracy, discussed in Chapter 2, would see the plea cynically. Like any bureaucrats, the IMF staff seeks to justify and maximize its budget.

Cynicism is justifiable, given the IMF's poor track record. While the changes the IMF is proposing at this juncture are new, the fact that the IMF is redefining its role in developing countries following a crisis is not new. The IMF always seems ready to adapt, but still does not seem to promote economic development.

Maybe it's time to stop looking at *how* the IMF can do better, and ask *why* the IMF should bother. That is, it is time to look at IMF incentives.

Reform of the IMF typically focuses on improving IMF policies: *How* can the IMF do a better job? One should also address, however, why it should bother to do better: *Why* should the IMF do a better job – what is in it for the IMF? Instead of tinkering with the increasing, the decreasing, the selling or the owning of policy conditionality, one should focus on the incentives of the IMF to lend and to enforce conditions in the first place.

This should not be surprising to the IMF staff – indeed, the importance of incentives is well known to them. When designing an economic program of reform, incentives are changed. This is the whole idea of economic reform. Why, then, is there not more discussion of changing the incentives of the IMF itself?

With respect to Fund incentives, de Rato's move to secure resources outside of lending may be a good decision. Public Choice theorists may bemoan the fact that at a time where resources are short, the IMF chooses to seek new sources of income instead of cutting its budget. But a non-lending source of revenue for the IMF may be preferable in the long run. At least it may lower the incentive to lend continuously to governments. Potentially, the IMF can go about the important business of surveillance and lend selectively only in crisis situations.

The IMF should not lend to generate income. Not only should the IMF have a non-lending source of income, perhaps this should be its only source of income, with any dividends from lending going to shareholders instead of IMF pockets and coffers.

Other perverse incentives the IMF faces – such as the incentive to follow international political pressures in its lending decisions – should also be addressed. In particular, perhaps the IMF Executive Board should be made independent of international political pressures, much as central bankers are made independent of domestic political pressures.

At present, the dominant critique of IMF governance regards representation. Presently, the governance of the IMF favors countries that do not participate in IMF programs. Ten of the 24 seats on the Executive Board are filled by Europeans – an eleventh is held by the US. As a first step to change the governance of the IMF, the Executive Board can be expanded so that there are more seats at the table for poor countries. In addition, many believe that the actual distribution of votes at the IMF should change. Even Managing Director de Rato supports the idea. Buira (Chapter 6) has proposed a formula by which governance at the IMF can be recalibrated. Under most proposals, however, the major shareholder's votes would not change very much – the US would still have the most voting power by far. But smaller industrialized countries, like Belgium or Denmark, would have their vote shares cut significantly. The windfall would go to emerging market countries, like China, Brazil, Mexico, and South Africa.

The question of whether IMF governance should be reformed, thus, rests on questions about who should have more say: Japan or China? Belgium or Brazil? A change in governance would promote role reversals among these types of countries. The very top (the US) and the very bottom (the poorest countries) would not change much.

So, would such governance reform make much difference with respect to international political influence over the IMF? Note that the

United States would still have the most votes and retain veto power over major IMF decisions, and there is evidence that besides the US, Germany, Japan, France, and the United Kingdom also use the IMF for political purposes. Anecdotal evidence abounds. More important than anecdotes, however, is the systematic evidence:

- Countries that prove themselves to be allies of the US by voting along with the super power on key issues at the UN are more likely to get an IMF loan. The US abuses its influence at the IMF to reward friends and punish enemies.
- Beyond just voting with the US, countries voting at the UN with the G-7 receive more IMF loans. Other powerful countries, like Japan, Germany, France, and the United Kingdom, also appear to abuse their influence at the IMF to reward friends and punish enemies.
- Temporary UN Security Council members are more likely to have an IMF arrangement than other countries. Powerful countries especially care about voting on the UN Security Council since it can take major decisions, like going to war, so the IMF is particularly abused to favor countries when they serve on this important body.
- US bank exposure and lending in a developing country is a determinant of both whether or not a country receives a loan, and the size of the loan. The US also uses its influence at the IMF to pursue financial interests.
- The more US foreign aid a country receives, the lighter punishments it receives from the IMF for noncompliance. Countries favored by the US in terms of its own foreign aid are also favored by the IMF in terms of enforcement of conditionality. Friends of the US are granted dispensations.
- The increasing length and detail of IMF arrangements allows for political discretion in the defining of "compliance" on a case by case basis. Recipient countries deemed important by the Fund's major shareholders are given leeway under this ambiguity.

There is no question that the IMF is abused for the purposes of international politics. But changing vote shares at the IMF would not change this. It would simply change *whose* political interests the IMF would serve. So, the IMF might be subject to less pressure from European countries, but it would receive new political pressure from countries like China. The actors might change but the basic political problem would remain.

Shifting vote shares is a reform of IMF governance that is weak with respect to international political pressures. Yet, how can one remove the incentive of the IMF to follow international political imperatives?

To prevent the abuse of the IMF, the main governing body of the IMF – the Executive Board – must be made independent.[2] Much like central bank presidents have been given independence domestically in many countries for the greater good of society, IMF Directors should be appointed for the kinds of terms that independent central bankers serve. The Directors who sit on the IMF Executive Board should be appointed for long, non-renewable terms, which do not coincide with the election cycles of the major shareholders. To the extent shareholders control the purse strings, they may still pressure the IMF for political reasons, but making the Executive Board independent is at least a step in the right direction. If the governance of the IMF is freed from pursuing foreign policy objectives, the institution might be able to function more closely to its mandate.

Such a reform is only likely if people can convince the major shareholders of the IMF that they are better off "tying their hands" than maintaining the present political control they have over the IMF. This is not impossible. It must be further demonstrated that (1) allies of the IMF's most powerful members are not forced to comply with conditionality, and (2) countries that do comply with IMF conditions fare better than those that do not. If US policy makers are convinced of this, they may recognize that – much like Ulysses had to bind himself to the mast of his ship so as not to be lured by the songs of the sirens – the US must bind itself with an independent IMF Executive Board to prevent itself from intervening in the activities of the IMF for political reasons.[3]

The basic idea is that while US allies may be better off in the short run receiving lenience from the IMF, they will be better off in the long run if they face a stricter IMF. Since politicians, who depend on winning elections, face short time horizons, they may be tempted to pursue short run interests. But an IMF independent of short run electoral pressures would be better able to resist short run temptation and could help developing countries for the long run.

Yet there is a long way to go before such a case can be made. More evidence is required to show that noncompliance due to political pressure is indeed the reason for IMF program failure. Many believe that noncompliance is not at all the reason IMF programs fail. IMF programs may also fail because IMF policy advice is bad.

And then there is also the problem of domestic politics. The single most consistent effect of IMF programs is the exacerbation of income inequality. This is probably not intended in most IMF arrangements, but is rather the result of domestic political realities – domestic elites pressure their own governments to structure IMF reforms in such a way to protect their interests, pushing the costs of economic reform on less fortunate groups of society.

Despite the IMF's recent renewed commitment to the poor, domestic political problems are difficult to overcome. Some might say that this is not the fault of the IMF. But to the extent that IMF conditionality is abused to justify policy changes that exacerbate income inequality, IMF conditionality bears part of the blame, because without the IMF the domestic political payoffs for policy change would be different.

Even extreme governance reform will not make the IMF a democratically accountable institution. Governance reform is no panacea for the problems of accountability that plague the IMF. The actions of the IMF staff are removed from the Executive Board, which in turn is far removed from the Board of Governors, which in turn is quite far removed from the direct control of the citizens of the world they supposedly represent. Ceding too much authority to the IMF is a recipe for continued abuse of the institution.

The IMF has chosen not to scale back its role in development. The current shortfall in resources is instead an opportunity to build a "stronger and multilaterally-engaged institution."[4] A recent Fund strategy review asserts that in emerging market countries, the IMF can "do more by way of crisis prevention and response."[5] As for poor countries, the IMF calls for "deeper but more focused engagement by the Fund."[6] More than 50 years of experience of conditional lending to the developing world does not appear to be enough to demonstrate that it does not work. This time, if better results are not forthcoming, the opinion of skeptical critics, who think the IMF should pull out of the development business, should not be forgotten. Otherwise, the reform of IMF conditionality will continue to move in Goldilocks-like circles – in the past there was too little conditionality, then too much conditionality, then too little … the IMF answer to critics always seems to be that they finally have it "just right."

The IMF is staffed by some of the world's best, brightest and well-intentioned economists who forgo lucrative private sector opportunities to dedicate their lives instead to improving the conditions of people in the developing world. But promoting economic development is no easy task, and, unfortunately, the IMF faces – perhaps insurmountable – obstacles in the form of international and domestic politics. For all of the IMF's efforts, levels of development in countries where the IMF is most deeply involved have been repressed. This is not simply because the IMF intervenes in the hardest cases – even accounting for this fact, the effect of IMF programs on economic growth is negative. The IMF involves itself in many developing countries on a routine basis, imposing conditionality for decades at a time. A scaled-back IMF, which imposes less conditionality and resists the temptation to lend, will do less harm. By restricting its lending activities to only the most severe crises, the IMF has the potential to do much good.

Notes

Introduction

1 The 49 countries participating as of January 30, 2005 are Albania, Argentina, Azerbaijan, Bangladesh, Bolivia, Brazil, Bulgaria, Burkina Faso, Burundi, Cape Verde, Chad, Colombia, Congo (Republic), Congo (Democratic Republic), Côte d'Ivoire, Croatia, Dominica, Dominican Republic, Gabon, Gambia, Georgia, Ghana, Guyana, Honduras, Kenya, Kyrgyz Republic, Laos, Madagascar, Mali, Mongolia, Mozambique, Nepal, Nicaragua, Niger, Paraguay, Peru, Romania, Rwanda, Senegal, Serbia and Montenegro, Sierra Leone, Sri Lanka, Tajikistan, Tanzania, Turkey, Uganda, Ukraine, Uruguay, and Zambia. Source: IMF, *IMF Annual Report* (Washington, DC: International Monetary Fund, 2003, 2004, 2005).

1 What is the IMF?

1 Representatives from 45 countries were present, but the Soviet Union did not sign.

2 For an excellent account of the development of the international monetary system from the nineteenth century to the end of the twentieth century, see Barry Eichengreen, *Globalizing Capital: A History of the International Monetary System* (Princeton, NJ: Princeton University Press, 1998). The characterization in this section of the origins of the IMF follows Eichengreen's account.

3 For example, see John Maynard Keynes, *The Collected Writings of John Maynard Keynes, Volume II, The Economic Consequences of the Peace* (London: Macmillan St. Martin's Press, 1971), 149–54.

4 Roy F. Harrod, *The Pound Sterling* (Princeton, NJ: Princeton Essays in International Finance 13, 1952), 3; cited in Eichengreen, *Globalizing Capital*, 97.

5 Entitled *Preliminary Draft Proposal for a United Nations Stabilization Fund and Bank for Reconstruction and Development of the United Nations and Associated Nations.*

6 Eichengreen, *Globalizing Capital*, 97.

7 Eichengreen, *Globalizing Capital*, 97. Today, instead of having reserves approximating half of the value of global imports, the IMF holds on reserve a total of less than 2 percent of global imports. See Thomas G.

Weiss, "Governance, Good Governance and Global Governance: Conceptual and Actual Challenges," *Third World Quarterly* 21 no. 5 (2000): 795–814.

8 Eichengreen, *Globalizing Capital*, 105 fn 23, 108.

9 See Beth A. Simmons, "The Legalization of International Monetary Affairs," *International Organization* 54 (2000): 573–602. This effect may be due to countries signing under convenient circumstances – a selection effect, as shown by Jana Von Stein, "Do Treaties Constrain or Screen? Selection Bias and Treaty Compliance," *American Political Science Review*, 99 no. 4 (2005): 611–622.

10 On the growth of membership of the IMF, see Chapter 19 of James M. Boughton, *Silent Revolution: The International Monetary Fund, 1979–1989* (Washington, DC: IMF, 2001).

11 IMF, *IMF Annual Report* (Washington, DC: IMF, 1950), 102; cited in Boughton, *Silent Revolution*, 965.

12 The 1976 *IMF Annual Report* (which provides data for April 30, 1975 through April 30, 1976), refers to this member as South Vietnam, even though the member was called Vietnam from 1956 to 1975. The 1977 *IMF Annual Report* then goes back, referring to this member as Viet Nam.

13 This meant, however, that Taiwan was no longer a member because China stipulates its participation in any international organization requires the organization not to recognize Taiwan.

14 A list of each member country, its representative governor, quota, and vote share is available at www.imf.org under "members."

15 As the Articles of Agreement (Article XII, Section 3(c)) explain, if the five appointed Directors "do not include the two members, the holdings of whose currencies by the Fund in the General Resources Account have been, on the average over the preceding two years, reduced below their quotas by the largest absolute amounts in terms of the special drawing right, either one or both of such members, as the case may be, may appoint an Executive Director."

16 Director Damian Ondo Mañe represents Benin, Burkina Faso, Cameroon, Cape Verde, Central African Republic, Chad, Comoros, Democratic Republic of Congo, Republic of Congo, Côte d'Ivoire, Djibouti, Equatorial Guinea, Gabon, Guinea, Guinea-Bissau, Madagascar, Mali, Mauritania, Mauritius, Niger, Rwanda, São Tomé and Príncipe, Senegal, and Togo.

17 There is no study I am aware of that considers how groups of countries come together to elect a Director.

18 Director Fritz Zurbrügg represents Azerbaijan, Kyrgyz Republic, Poland, Serbia and Montenegro, Switzerland, Tajikistan, Turkmenistan, and Uzbekistan.

19 The G-7 is an informal group of seven economically influential countries: the United States, Japan, Germany, United Kingdom, France, Italy, and Canada.

20 The mathematical details behind this claim can be found in: James Raymond Vreeland, "IMF Executive Director Voting Power," Unpublished manuscript, Politics Department, New York University. On voting power in general, see L. S. Shapley and Martin Shubik, "A Method for Evaluating the Distribution of Power in a Committee System," *American Political Science Review* 48 no. 3 (1954): 787–92.

21 David D. Driscoll, *What is the International Monetary Fund?* (Washington, DC: External Relations Department, IMF, 1997), 9.

22 J. Lawrence Broz and Michael Brewster Hawes, "Congressional Politics of Financing the IMF," *International Organization* 60 no. 1 (Spring 2006): 367–99.

23 Frank Southard, *The Evolution of the International Monetary Fund,* Essay in International Finance No. 135 (Princeton, NJ: Princeton University, 1979). Cited in Strom Thacker, "The High Politics of IMF Lending," *World Politics* 52 no. 1 (1999): 38–75.

24 Personal conversation with Anne O. Krueger, First Deputy Managing Director of the IMF (26 March 2003).

25 Sometimes the IMF makes loans when a country is not in crisis – the IMF provides, for example, "precautionary" loans for countries that do not presently have a balance of payments problem, if the country is undergoing painful economic reforms and the IMF anticipates that the government might require a line of credit in the near future. The vast majority of IMF loans, however, go to countries that are in some kind of economic crisis.

26 This account follows Lawrence J. McQuillan and Peter C. Montgomery, *The International Monetary Fund, Financial Medic to the World? A Primer on Mission, Operations, and Public Policy Issues,* (Stanford, CA: Hoover Institution Press, 1999), 63; who follow Louis W. Pauly, *Who Elected the Bankers? Surveillance and Control in the World Economy,* (Ithaca, NY: Cornell University Press, 1997), 83.

27 Letter dated January 26, 1944, published in J. Keith Horsefield, *International Monetary Fund, 1945–1965: Twenty Years of International Monetary Cooperation, Volume 1: Chronicle* (Washington, DC: IMF, 1969), 74.

28 Horsefield, *International Monetary Fund, 1945–1965,* 74.

29 Ironically, the British government itself faced a heavy-handed IMF, which imposed strict conditions on the United Kingdom when it entered into an IMF economic program on December 31, 1975. See Mark D. Harmon, *The British Labour Government and the 1976 IMF Crisis* (New York: St. Martin's Press, 1997).

30 The amendment was: "The Fund shall adopt policies on the use of its resources that will assist members to solve their balance of payments problems" (IMF, *IMF Annual Report* (Washington, DC: IMF, 1968), 155). See also Scott R. Sidell, *The IMF and Third-World Political Instability: Is There a Connection?* (New York: St. Martin's Press, 1988), 5.

31 France was operating a discriminatory dual exchange rate, offering a higher rate to the United States to restore dollar reserves, which caused negative externalities by lowering imports to the US from other countries. See Eichengreen, *Globalizing Capital,* 104.

32 The *IMF Annual Report* of 1953 explains that loans would be provided so that "members should find it possible, without risking a loss of reserves, *to modify their policies so as to conform more closely to the Fund's objectives.*" (IMF, *IMF Annual Report* (Washington, DC: IMF, 1953), 52 emphasis added). The *IMF Annual Report* of 1954 further elaborated that while these Stand-by Arrangements were intended to last just six months, "the Fund will give sympathetic consideration to a request for a longer stand-by arrangement in the light of the problems facing the member *and the measures being taken to deal with them*" (IMF, *IMF Annual Report* (Washington, DC: IMF, *1954*), 131 emphasis added).

33 The IMF also had a Stand-by Arrangement with Mexico this year.
34 Sarah Babb and Ariel Buira, "Mission Creep, Mission Push and Discretion: The Case of IMF Conditionality," in Ariel Buira, *The IMF and the World Bank at Sixty* (London: Anthem Press 2005), 59–84.
35 For a more technical yet still quite accessible description of the IMF approach to financial programming, see Graham Bird, "The IMF: A Bird's Eye View of Its Role and Operations," *Journal of Economic Surveys* (Forthcoming 2007).
36 IMF, *IMF Annual Report* (Washington, DC: IMF, 1979), 137.
37 Executive Board Decision No. 6056-(79/38) of 2 March 1979, published in the *IMF Annual Report 1979*. Also see A. W. Hooke, *The International Monetary Fund, Its Evolution, Organization, and Activities* (Washington, DC: IMF), 37–40.
38 Jacques J. Polak, *The Changing Nature of IMF Conditionality*, Essay in International Finance No. 184 (Princeton, NJ: Princeton University, 1991).
39 Graham Bird, "IMF Programmes: Is There a Conditionality Laffer Curve?" *World Economics* 2 (2001): 29–49. On the increasing number of IMF conditions, also see Axel Dreher and Roland Vaubel, "The Causes and Consequences of IMF Conditionality," *Emerging Markets Finance and Trade* 40 no. 3 (2004): 26–54; and Axel Dreher, "IMF Conditionality: Theory and Evidence," Prepared for the Independent Evaluation Office (IEO) of the IMF in connection with its study on structural conditionality (2006).
40 For a good and accessible history of the East Asian financial crisis and its aftermath, see Paul Blustein, *The Chastening: Inside the Crisis that Rocked the Global Financial System and Humbled the IMF* (New York: Public Affairs, 2001).
41 A prominent proponent of this view is Jeffrey Sachs. See, among many examples, Jeffrey Sachs, "How to Run the International Monetary Fund," *Foreign Affairs* (July–August, 2004): 60–4.
42 See "What is the International Monetary Fund" under www.imf.org. The version cited here was updated July 30, 2004: www.imf.org/external/pubs/ft/exrp/what.htm.
43 IMF, "Conditionality in Fund-Supported Programs – Policy Issues," Prepared by the Policy Development and Review Department (in consultation with other departments), approved by Jack Boorman (16 February 2001).
44 The argument of the late economist James Tobin of Yale University, which is covered in Chapter 6, notwithstanding.
45 Hooke, *The International Monetary Fund*, 47–8.
46 In fact, even without signing an IMF agreement, Shagari was eventually overthrown in a coup d'état in part because he appeared to be bowing to the IMF.
47 For more on the unconditioned lending facilities, see the IMF website (www.imf.org) under "lending facilities," which describes the Supplemental Reserve Facility, the Compensatory Financing Facility, and Emergency assistance.
48 *IMF Annual Report 1953*: 52.
49 *IMF Annual Report 1953*: 50. Note that while the first IMF loan was with France in 1947, this was not under a Stand-by Arrangement. Even the

original loan with France, however, had a small degree of conditionality, as mentioned earlier.

50 *IMF Annual Report* (2005: 112).

51 Joseph Gold, *The Stand-by Arrangements of the International Monetary Fund: A Commentary on Their Formal, Legal, and Financial Aspects* (Washington, DC: IMF, 1970), 47.

52 Decision No. 6056-(79/38), 2 March 1979. Published in *Selected Decisions and Selected Documents of the International Monetary Fund Nineteenth Issue*, (Washington, DC: IMF 1994), 85. Also see Decision No 2603-(68/132), Sept. 20, 1968: "language having a contractual flavor will be avoided in the stand-by documents." Published in Gold, *The Stand-by Arrangements of the International Monetary Fund*, 251–2.

53 Gold, *The Stand-by Arrangements of the International Monetary Fund*, 47.

54 The document, which is the property of Pakistan, is available on the IMF website by agreement with Pakistan. The document along with some of the commentary was also published by James Raymond Vreeland, "Pakistan's Debt of Gratitude," *Foreign Policy Magazine* (March–April, 2002): 72–3.

2 Who controls the IMF?

1 David D. Driscoll, *What is the International Monetary Fund?* (Washington, DC: External Relations Department, IMF, 1997), 8.

2 Roland Vaubel, "Bureaucracy at the IMF and the World Bank: A Comparison of the Evidence," *World Economy* 19 no. 2 (1996): 195–210.

3 Roland Vaubel, "A Public Choice Approach to International Organization," *Public Choice* 51 no. 1 (1986): 39–57. For an empirical test see Roland Vaubel, Axel Dreher, and Ugurlu Soylu, "Staff Growth in International Organizations: A Principal-Agent Problem? An Empirical Analysis," in John-ren Chen and David Sapsford, *Principles of International Institutions – Theoretical Foundations and Empirical Evidence* (New York: Edward Elgar Publishing 2006).

4 Vaubel, "Bureaucracy at the IMF and the World Bank." Also see Roland Vaubel, "The Political Economy of the International Monetary Fund: A Public Choice Analysis," in Roland Vaubel and Thomas Willett, *The Political Economy of International Organizations: A Public Choice Approach* (Boulder, CO: Westview Press, 1991): 204 – 44.

5 Press Release, *IMF Survey* (1994): 222 emphasis added.

6 Thomas Willett, "Upping the Ante for Political Economy Analysis of the International Financial Institutions," *World Economy* 24 no. 3 (2001): 317–32.

7 Sarah Babb and Ariel Buira, "Mission Creep, Mission Push and Discretion: The Case of IMF Conditionality," in Ariel Buira, *The IMF and the World Bank at Sixty* (London: Anthem Press 2005).

8 See Strom Thacker, "The High Politics of IMF Lending," *World Politics* 52 no. 1 (1999), 41, who cites Samuel Lichtensztejn and Mónica Baer, *Fondo Monetario Internacional y Banco Mundial: Estrategias y Políticas del Poder Financiero* (Mexico City: Ediciones de Cultura Popular, 1987): 60–1. Also see Miles Kahler, "The United States and the International Monetary Fund," in Margaret P. Karns and Karen A. Mingst, *The*

United States and Multilateral Institutions (Boston, MA: Unwin Hyman, 1990).

9 For example, see Cheryl Payer, *The Debt Trap: The International Monetary Fund and the Third World* (New York: Monthly Review Press, 1974); and Richard Swedberg, "The Doctrine of Economic Neutrality of the IMF and the World Bank," *Journal of Peace Research* 23 no. 4 (1986), cited in Thacker "The High Politics of IMF Lending," 40.

10 Bessma Momani, "American Politicization of the International Monetary Fund," *Review of International Political Economy* 11 (5 December 2004): 880–904.

11 Bessma Momani, "The IMF, the US War on Terrorism, and Pakistan," *Asian Affairs* 31, no. 1 (2004): 41–50.

12 Tony Killick, *IMF Programs in Developing Countries: Design and Impact* (London: Routledge, 1995), 118–19.

13 See Kendall W. Stiles, *Negotiating Debt: The IMF Lending Process*, (Boulder, CO: Westview Press, 1991).

14 Graham Bird and Dane Rowlands "IMF Lending: How is it Affected by Economic, Political and Institutional Factors?" *Journal of Policy Reform* 4 no. 4 (2001): 243–70.

15 Randall W. Stone, "Lending Credibility in Africa," *American Political Science Review* 98 no. 4 (2004): 577–91. Randall W. Stone, *Lending Credibility: The International Monetary Fund and the Post-Communist Transition* (Princeton, NJ: Princeton University Press, 2002).

16 These findings have important implications for compliance, as will be discussed in Chapter 5.

17 Stone, *Lending Credibility*, 62.

18 Axel Dreher and Nathan M. Jensen, "Independent Actor or Agent? An Empirical Analysis of the Impact of US Interests on IMF Conditions," *The Journal of Law and Economics* 50 no. 1 (forthcoming 2007).

19 Axel Dreher and Jan-Egbert Sturm, "Do IMF and World Bank Influence Voting in the UN General Assembly?" KOF Working Paper 137, ETH Zurich (2006).

20 Axel Dreher, Jan-Egbert Sturm, and James Vreeland, "Does Membership on the UN Security Council Influence IMF Decisions? Evidence from Panel Data," Leitner Working Paper 2006–11 (2006).

21 J. Lawrence Broz and Michael Brewster Hawes, "U.S. Domestic Politics and International Monetary Fund Policy," in Darren Hawkins, David A. Lake, Daniel Nielson, and Michael J. Tierney, *Delegation and Agency in International Organizations* (New York: Cambridge University Press, forthcoming 2006).

22 The effect of money-center bank campaign contributions and skill-levels of voters are surprisingly statistically significant even when Broz and Hawes account for other factors. For example, they hold constant the political party of the representative, which is important because Republicans have generally opposed contributions to the IMF, while Democrats have tended to support them.

23 Thomas Oatley and Jason Yackee, "American Interests and IMF Lending," *International Politics* 41 no. 3 (2004): 415–29.

24 Erica Gould, "Money Talks: Supplementary Financiers and International Monetary Fund Conditionality," *International Organization* 57 no.3 (2003): 551–86.

25 Gould, "Money Talks," 564.

26 The finding concerning US financing was not statistically significant when certain control variables were included, but the finding concerning private financial institutions was statistically significant.

27 Gould, "Money Talks," 564.

3 Why do governments participate in IMF programs?

1 The formal definition of balance of payments deficit used by the IMF is presented below in Chapter 5.

2 Studies that did find that increasing the balance of payments deficit significantly predicts participation include Julio A. Santaella, "Stylized Facts Before IMF-Supported Adjustment," *IMF Staff Papers* 43 (September 1996): 502–44; and Morris Goldstein and Peter J. Montiel, "Evaluating Fund Stabilization Programs with Multicountry Data: Some Methodological Pitfalls," *IMF Staff Papers* 33 (June 1986): 304–44.

3 The following studies have not found that the balance of payments is a statistically significant predictor of IMF program participation: Malcolm Knight and Julio A. Santaella, "Economic Determinants of Fund Financial Arrangements," *Journal of Development Economics* 54 no. 2 (1997): 405–36; Patrick Conway, "IMF Lending Programs: Participation and Impact," *Journal of Development Economics* 45 no. 2 (1994): 365–91; and Sebastian Edwards and Julio A. Santaella, "Devaluation Controversies in the Developing Countries: Lessons from the Bretton Woods Era," in Michael D. Bordo and Barry Eichengreen, *A Retrospective on the Bretton Woods System* (Chicago, IL: University of Chicago Press 1993), 405–55.

4 These data are available electronically on CD-ROM and on the Internet through the World Bank (www.worldbank.org).

5 The fact that data are not missing at random is problem addressed in a recent unpublished study: B. Peter Rosendorff and James Raymond Vreeland, "Democracy and Data Dissemination: The Effect of Political Regime on Transparency."

6 A review of statistical studies of participation in IMF programs reports that there is consensus in the literature on the effect of this factor: low levels of foreign reserves predicts IMF participation. Graham Bird, "The International Monetary Fund and Developing Countries: A Review of the Evidence and Policy Options," *International Organization* 50 no. 3 (1996): 477–511.

7 Measured as the annual average in terms of monthly imports.

8 For examples, see Conway "IMF Lending Programs"; Santaella, "Stylized Facts Before IMF-Supported Adjustment"; Knight and Santaella, "Economic Determinants of Fund Financial Arrangements"; Adam Przeworski and James Raymond Vreeland, "The Effect of IMF Programs on Economic Growth," *The Journal of Development Economics* 62 no. 2 (2000): 385–421.

9 Bird, "The International Monetary Fund and Developing Countries," cites the studies of Louis M. Goreux, "The Fund and Low Income Countries,"

in Catherine Gwin and Richard Feinberg, *The International Monetary Fund in a Multipolar World: Pulling Together, US-Third World Policy Perspectives, 13* (Washington, DC: Overseas Development Council, 1989); Tony Killick, Moazzam Malik and Marcus Manuel, "What Can We Know About the Effects of IMF Programmes?" *World Economy* 15 no. 5 (1992): 575–97; Graham Bird, *IMF Lending to Developing Countries, Issues and Evidence* (London: Routledge, 1995); Conway "IMF Lending Programs: Participation and Impact"; and Knight and Santaella, "Economic Determinants of Fund Financial Arrangements."

10 Graham Bird, "Borrowing from the IMF: The Policy Implications of Recent Empirical Research," *World Development* 24 no. 11 (1996): 1759.

11 Note that this figure includes spells that may continue beyond the year 2000. So we know that the average duration of participation was at least 5.5 years. History may yet prove that the average is higher.

12 1985 PPP dollars. Source: Alan Heston and Robert Summers, *Penn World Tables 5.6* (Cambridge: National Bureau of Economic Research, 1995); and World Bank, *World Development Indicators* (Washington, DC: The World Bank, 2005).

13 See for example Nouriel Roubini and Brad Setser, "Breaking the IMF Habit," *Foreign Policy* (November/December 2004): 84–5; and Graham Bird, "The IMF Forever: An Analysis of the Prolonged Use of Fund Resources," *Journal of Development Studies* 40 no. 6 (August 2004): 30–58.

14 Robert J. Barro and Jong-Wha Lee, "IMF programs: Who is chosen and what are the effects?" *Journal of Monetary Economics* 52 no. 7 (October 2005): 1245–69.

15 See Karen L. Remmer, "The Politics of Economic Stabilization, IMF Standby Programs in Latin America, 1954–84," *Comparative Politics* 19 no. 1 (1986): 6.

16 Quentin Peel, "Debt and democracy," *Financial Times* (16 August 1983): 8.

17 Edward A. Gargan, "Nigerians Debate a Proposed Loan," *New York Times* (6 October 1985): 17.

18 Edward A. Gargan, "Nigeria Leader Wary on IMF Loan," *New York Times* (8 October 1985): A8.

19 Edward A. Gargan, "Nigeria's Economy Faces New Burden," *New York Times* (27 January 1986): D1.

20 Financial Desk, "Accord Reported on Nigerian Loan," *New York Times* (1 October 1986): D23.

21 Quentin Peel, "Debt and Democracy," 8.

22 Remmer, "The Politics of Economic Stabilization," 7, 21.

23 Edwards and Santaella, "Devaluation Controversies in the Developing Countries," 425.

24 Roland Vaubel, "A Public Choice Approach to International Organization," *Public Choice* 51 no. 1 (1986), 45.

25 Alastair Smith and James Raymond Vreeland, "The Survival of Political Leaders and IMF Programs," in Gustav Ranis, James Raymond Vreeland, and Stephen Kosack, *Globalization and the Nation State: The Impact of the IMF and the World Bank* (New York: Routledge 2006): 263 – 89.

26 Among several studies they have published, see Graham Bird and Dane Rowlands, "Financing Balance of Payments Adjustment: Options in Light

of the Elusive Catalytic Effect of IMF Lending," *Comparative Economic Studies* 46 no. 3 (2004): 468–86.

27 Nathan Jensen, "Crisis, Conditions, and Capital: the Effect of International Monetary Fund Agreements on Foreign Direct Investment Inflows," *Journal of Conflict Resolution* 48 no. 2 (2004): 194–210.

28 Nancy Brune, Geoffrey Garrett, and Bruce Kogut, "The International Monetary Fund and the Global Spread of Privatization," *IMF Staff Papers* 51 (July 2004).

29 Susan Schadler, *IMF Conditionality: Experiences Under Stand-By and Extended Arrangements, Part II: Background Papers, Occasional Paper 129* (Washington, DC: International Monetary Fund, 1995).

30 Thomas M. Callaghy, "Globalization and Marginalization: Debt and the International Underclass," *Current History* 96/613 (1997): 392–6; Thomas M. Callaghy, "Networks and Governance in Africa: Innovation in the Debt Regime," in Thomas M. Callaghy, Ronald Kassimir, and Robert Latham, *Intervention and Transnationalism in Africa: Global-Local Networks of Power* (New York: Cambridge University Press, 2002), 115–48; and Vinod K. Aggarwal, *Debt Games* (New York: Cambridge University Press, 1996).

31 Randall W. Stone, "Lending Credibility in Africa," *American Political Science Review* 98 no. 4 (2004); Martin S. Edwards, "Things Fall Apart: Why Do IMF Agreements Break Down?" Prepared for delivery at the Duke University Center for International Studies Conference International Institutions: Global Processes/Domestic Consequences, Durham, April 9–11, 1999.

32 Stanley Fischer, "On the Need for an International Lender of Last Resort," prepared for delivery at the joint luncheon of the American Economic Association and the American Finance Association, New York (3 January 1999).

33 Robert D. Putnam, "Diplomacy and Domestic Politics: the Logic of Two-Level Games," *International Organization* 42 (1988): 457.

34 Luigi Spaventa, "Two Letters of Intent: External Crises and Stabilization Policy, Italy, 1973–77," in John Williamson, *IMF Conditionality* (Washington, DC: Institute for International Economics 1983): 441–73.

35 James Bjork, "The Uses of Conditionality," *East European Quarterly* 29 (1995): 89.

36 Avinash K. Dixit, *The Making of Economic Policy: A Transaction-Cost Politics Perspective* (Cambridge, MA: MIT Press, 1996), 85.

37 Thomas C. Schelling, *The Strategy of Conflict* (Cambridge: Harvard University Press, 1960), 22.

38 Allen Drazen, "Conditionality and Ownership in IMF Lending: A Political Economy Approach," *IMF Staff Papers* 49 (November 2002): 36–67.

39 This does not mean that enforcement of IMF conditions is perfect. Indeed, there are many anecdotes of the IMF relaxing conditions or continuing to extend credit to a country that has not fully complied with an IMF agreement. But, as others have shown, noncompliance is often sanctioned. Chapter 5 will return to the question of compliance.

40 Louis W. Pauly, *Who Elected the Bankers? Surveillance and Control in the World Economy* (Ithaca, NY: Cornell University Press, 1997), 163–4. At the time of this publication, Pauly did not name the developing country to

hold the identities of the actors involved in confidence. He later revealed at an academic conference of political scientists, after the actors involved had long since left power, that the developing country in question was Pakistan. The conference was the 2001 Annual Meeting of the American Political Science Association held in San Francisco, California.

41 Andrew Kiondo, "The Nature of Economic Reforms in Tanzania," in Horace Campbell and Howard Stein, *Tanzania and the IMF: The Dynamics of Liberalization* (Boulder, CO: Westview Press 1992), 24–8, 35.

42 *Reuters*, 9 November 1998.

43 *Associated Press*, 5 November 1998.

44 Personal conversation with President Cardoso (31 March 2006).

45 For the details of this case, see James Raymond Vreeland, *The IMF and Economic Development* (New York: Cambridge University Press, 2003), 39–51.

46 George Tsebelis, "Decision Making in Political Systems," *British Journal of Political Science* 25 no. 3 (1995): 289–326. George Tsebelis, *Veto Players: How Political Institutions Work* (Princeton, NJ: Princeton University Press, 2002).

47 This is a simplification of the full argument of Tsebelis (cited above).

48 This is a simplification of the range of variation across political systems. Sometimes, for example, there are coalition governments under presidential systems. See Adam Przeworski, José Cheibub, and Sebastian Saiegh, "Government Coalitions and Legislative Success Under Presidentialism and Parliamentarism," *British Journal of Political Science* 34 no. 4 (2004): 565–87.

49 To be more precise, the probability does not decrease. Note, furthermore, that the ideal points of veto players may be correlated, so the resistance to policy change may increase at a decreasing rate. In other words, the effect of adding a second veto player has a greater impact than adding a third, which has more impact than a fourth, etc. So, there may be diminishing returns from additional veto players. To capture diminishing returns from additional veto players, I use the natural logarithm of the number of veto players when testing the argument statistically in the following subsection.

50 The data for number of veto players comes from Thorsten Beck, George Clarke, Alberto Groff, Philip Keefer, and Patrick Walsh, *New Tools and New Tests in Comparative Political Economy: The Database of Political Institutions* (Groff, Switzerland: Federal Department of Foreign Affairs, 1999). The definition of the number of veto players is somewhat tedious. The basic idea is to count actors (individual or collective) who have a formal or institutionalized influence on the policy making process. The longer definition goes as follows: The variable is coded 1 in countries where the legislature is not competitively elected. In presidential democracies the variable is the sum of: 1 for the chief executive, 1 if the chief executive is competitively elected, 1 if the opposition controls the legislature, 1 for each chamber of the legislature (unless the president's party has a majority in the lower house and a closed list system is in effect, implying stronger presidential control of his/her party, and therefore of the legislature), and 1 for each party coded as allied with the president's party and which has an ideological orientation closer to that of the main opposition party than to that of the president's party. In parliamentary democracies, the variable is the sum of: 1 for the chief executive, 1 if the chief executive

is competitively elected, 1 if the opposition controls the legislature, 1 for every party in the government coalition (as long as the parties are needed to maintain a majority), 1 for every party in the government coalition that has a position on economic issues closer to the largest opposition party than to the party of the executive (the prime minister's party is not counted as a check if there is a closed rule in place – the prime minister is presumed in this case to control the party fully). Note that the variable does not count the innumerable actors who might have *informal* influence on policy making – this is not because these actors are not important, but because it is harder to code them in a systematic fashion. The goal here is to see if just this measure of resistance to policy change is correlated with IMF participation.

51 PPP stands for "Purchasing Power Parity." This indicates that the measure of per capita income accounts for the fact that non-traded goods and services, such as haircuts, may have similar values in different countries, even though the price, according to nominal exchange rates, may be very different. Chapter 6 further explains the concept.

52 This could be because when there are so many veto players in the political system the government cannot commit to enough reform – even if it had the leverage of an IMF arrangement – to please the IMF and conclude an arrangement. I discuss this possibility in detail in James Raymond Vreeland, "Institutional Determinants of IMF Agreements," Yale University Department of Political Science, mimeo (2002).

53 Still, this test is relatively unsophisticated compared with other studies. See for example Vreeland, *The IMF and Economic Development*, Chapter 3.

54 Note that a recent study specifies this effect further. Robert Trudel, a graduate of Yale University who published his senior essay on the IMF, shows that the effect of foreign reserves on IMF participation depends on a country's exchange rate regime. Countries with a floating exchange rate need not borrow from the IMF to shore up the value of the national currency, and so foreign reserves are not as strong a predictor of IMF participation. For the many developing countries that do have a fixed exchange rate, however, foreign reserves are a strong predictor of IMF participation. See Robert Trudel, "Effects of Exchange Rate Regime on IMF Program Participation," *Review of Policy Research* 22 no. 6 (2005): 919–36.

4 What are the effects of IMF programs?

1 Following in the footsteps of the East Asian financial crisis, Argentina defaulted on debt, the Argentine peso was devalued, and inflation, unemployment and poverty rose. IMF assistance did not help, and was suspended.

2 The Mexico peso faced a crisis when President Ernesto Zedillo's administration attempted to address the currency's overvaluation by relaxing currency controls, following the record deficit spending and corruption of the outgoing administration of Carlos Salinas. The US and the IMF led a nearly 50 billion dollar loan package that successfully stabilized the declining value of the peso. The success was remarkable: The Zedillo Administration saw that the loans were repaid by 1997 – ahead of schedule.

3 Kenya was a regular participant in IMF programs throughout the 1980s, entering into separate arrangements in 1980, 1982, 1983, 1985, 1988, and 1989.

4 IMF arrangements were also business as usual for Poland in the early 1990s, signing separate arrangements in 1990, 1991, 1993, and 1994. The last arrangement did not expire until March 1996.

5 As discussed in Chapter 1, the first negotiations for an IMF arrangement were with Finland in 1951, although the first signed arrangement was by Belgium in 1952.

6 African countries did not participate in IMF programs upon independence in part because of aid from European powers, and in part because the newly independent countries closely guarded their new independence and did not want to submit to IMF conditionality.

7 World Bank, *World Development Indicators on CD-ROM* (Washington, DC: The World Bank, 2004).

8 Chapter 3 only addresses the probability of *entering* into IMF programs. A full selection model would also involve estimating the probability of *continuing* participation as well.

9 Graham Bird, "The Effectiveness of Conditionality and the Political Economy of Policy Reform: Is it Simply a Matter of Political Will?" *Journal of Policy Reform* 1 no. 1 (1998): 90.

10 For a discussion, see Bird, "The Effectiveness of Conditionality and the Political Economy of Policy Reform"; also see Joan Nelson, *Economic Crisis and Policy Choice* (Princeton, NJ: Princeton University Press, 1991).

11 Norman K. Humphreys, *Historical Dictionary of the International Monetary Fund, Second Edition* (Lanham, MD: Scarecrow Press, 1999), 17–18.

12 For more, see IMF, *International Financial Statistics* (Washington DC: International Monetary Fund, published monthly).

13 See, for example, Graham Bird, "IMF Programs: Do They Work? Can They be Made to Work Better?" *World Development* 29 no. 11 (2001): 1849–65; and Nadeem Ul Haque and Mohsin S. Khan, "Do IMF-supported Programs Work? A survey of the cross-country empirical evidence," IMF Working Paper 98/169 (1998).

14 See Manuel Pastor, *The International Monetary Fund and Latin America: Economic Stabilization and Class Conflict* (Boulder, CO: Westview Press, 1987); and Manuel Pastor, "The Effects of IMF Programs in the Third World: Debate and Evidence from Latin America," *World Development* 15 no. 2 (1987): 365–91.

15 Tony Killick, Moazzam Malik, and Marcus Manuel, "What Can We Know About the Effects of IMF Programmes?" *World Economy* 15 no. 5 (1992).

16 Thorvaldur Gylfason, *Credit Policy and Economic Activity in Developing Countries with IMF Stabilization Programs*, Essay in International Finance No. 60 (Princeton, NJ: Princeton University, Department of Economics, 1987).

17 Mohsin S. Khan, "The Macroeconomic Effects of Fund-Supported Adjustment Programs," *IMF Staff Papers* 37 (1990): 195–234.

18 Patrick Conway, "IMF Lending Programs: Participation and Impact," *Journal of Development Economics* 45 no. 2 (1994).

19 Morris Goldstein and Peter J. Montiel, "Evaluating Fund Stabilization Programs with Multicountry Data: Some Methodological Pitfalls," *IMF Staff Papers* 33 (June 1986).

20 Several studies found no effect. Regarding the overall BOP, for example, see Thomas M. Reichmann and Richard T. Stillson, "Experience with Programs of Balance of Payments Adjustment: Stand-by Arrangements in the Highest

Tranches, 1963–72," *IMF Staff Papers* 25 (June 1978): 292–310; and Thomas A. Connors, "The Apparent Effects of Recent IMF Stabilization Programs," International Finance Discussion Papers 135, Board of Governors of the Federal Reserve System (1979). Regarding the current account, for example, see Pastor, "The Effects of IMF Programs in the Third World."

21 See, for example, Axel Dreher, "Does the IMF Influence Fiscal and Monetary Policy?" *The Journal of Policy Reform* 8 no. 3 (2005): 225–38.

22 Independent Evaluation Office, *Evaluation Report: Fiscal Adjustment in IMF-Supported Programs* (Washington, DC: International Monetary Fund, 2003).

23 Independent Evaluation Office, *Evaluation Report: Fiscal Adjustment in IMF-Supported Programs*, 30.

24 IMF, *First Annual Meeting of the Board of Governors, Report of the Executive Directors and Summary Proceedings, September 27 to October 3, 1946* (Washington, DC: International Monetary Fund, 1946), 25 (emphasis added), cited in Vreeland, *The IMF and Economic Development*, 2.

25 Horst Köhler, "Concluding Remarks by Horst Köhler, Chairman of the Executive Board and Managing Director of the International Monetary Fund at the Closing Joint Session," Prague, 27 September 2000.

26 For a summary, see IMF, "Conditionality in Fund-Supported Programs – Policy Issues." Widely cited before-after studies include Reichmann and Stillson, "Experience with Programs of Balance of Payments Adjustment: Stand-by Arrangements in the Highest Tranches, 1963–72"; and Pastor, "The Effects of IMF Programs in the Third World."

27 Haque and Khan, "Do IMF-supported programs work?"

28 Louis Dicks-Mireaux, Mauro Mecagni, and Susan Schadler, "Evaluating the effect of IMF lending to low income countries," *Journal of Development Economics* 61 no. 2 (2000): 495–526.

29 Adam Przeworski and James Raymond Vreeland, "The Effect of IMF Programs on Economic Growth," *The Journal of Development Economics* 62 no. 2 (2000).

30 Michael M. Hutchison and Ilan Noy, "Macroeconomic Effects of IMF-sponsored Programs in Latin America: Output Costs, Program Recidivism and the Vicious Cycle of Failed Stabilization," *Journal of International Money and Finance* 22 no. 7 (2003): 91–1014.

31 Barro and Jong-Wha Lee, "IMF Programs: Who is Chosen and What are the Effects?"

32 Axel Dreher, "IMF and Economic Growth: The Effects of Programs, Loans, and Compliance with Conditionality," *World Development* 34 no. 5 (2006): 769–88.

33 Vito Tanzi, "Fiscal Policy, Growth, and the Design of Stabilization Programs," in Mario I. Blejer and Ke-young Chu, *Fiscal Policy, Stabilization, and Growth in Developing Countries* (Washington, DC: IMF, 1989), 13–32. See also Vito Tanzi and Hamid Davoodi, *Roads to Nowhere: How Corruption in Public Investment Hurts Growth* (Washington, DC: International Monetary Fund, 1998).

34 Pastor, *The International Monetary Fund and Latin America*, 89.

35 Gopal Garuda, "The Distributional Effects of IMF Programs: A Cross-Country Analysis," *World Development* 28 no. 6 (2000): 1031–51.

36 The Gini coefficient potentially ranges from 0 (perfect equality, where everyone in a country shares the same level of income) to 1 (perfect

inequality, where a dictator dominates all income). In actuality the measure ranges from around 0.25 for egalitarian countries like Cyprus, Czech Republic, Denmark, Japan, Belgium, Sweden, and Norway to over 0.55 for countries with a great deal of income inequality like Honduras, Georgia, Colombia, and Panama.

37 James Raymond Vreeland, "The Effect of IMF Programs on Labor," *World Development* 30 no. 1 (2002): 121–39.
38 Pastor, *The International Monetary Fund and Latin America*, 54.
39 Garuda, "The Distributional Effects of IMF Programs," 1033.
40 Pastor, *The International Monetary Fund and Latin America*, 54.
41 Omotunde Johnson and Joanne Salop, "Distributional Aspects of Stabilization Programs in Developing Countries," *IMF Staff Papers* 27 (March 1980): 1–23.
42 Johnson and Salop, "Distributional Aspects of Stabilization Programs in Developing Countries," 12.
43 Garuda, "The Distributional Effects of IMF Programs," 1034.
44 Johnson and Salop, "Distributional Aspects of Stabilization Programs in Developing Countries," 23.
45 William Easterly, "The Effect of World Bank and IMF Programs on Poverty," in M. Dooley and J. Frankel, *Managing Currency Crises in Emerging Markets* (Chicago, IL: University of Chicago Press, 2003).
46 Independent Evaluation Office, *Evaluation Report: Fiscal Adjustment in IMF-Supported Programs*; and Ricardo Martin and Alex Segura-Ubiergo, *Social Spending in IMF-Supported Programs*, (Washington, DC: International Monetary Fund, 2004).
47 The studies also cite Sanjeev Gupta, Louis Dicks-Mireaux, Ritha Khemani, Calvin McDonald, and Marijn Verhoeven, "Social Issues in IMF-Supported Programs," IMF Occasional Paper No. 191 (2000). This study of 107 countries with IMF programs during 1985 to 1997 shows that spending on health and education increased in 65 of them.
48 Irfan Nooruddin and Joel W. Simmons, "The Politics of Hard Choices: IMF Programs and Government Spending," *International Organization* 60 no. 4 (2006).

5 Do governments comply with IMF programs?

1 Portions of this chapter come from James Raymond Vreeland, "IMF Program Compliance: Aggregate Index versus Policy Specific Research Strategies," *The Review of International Organizations* 1 no. 4 (2006).
2 Another possibility outside of this stark left-right presentation device is that (1) countries fail to comply, (2) IMF loans subsidize bad policies, (3) and the IMF also imposes bad policies of its own. This possibility is supported by evidence of Dreher's study discussed later in the chapter.
3 See, for example, Tony Killick, *IMF Programs in Developing Countries: Design and Impact* (London: Routledge, 1995). Many have used similar measures since, e.g. Michael Mussa and Miguel Savastano, "The IMF Approach to Economic Stabilization," in Ben S. Bernanke and Julio J. Rotemberg, *NBER Macroeconomics Annual 1999* (Cambridge, MA: MIT Press, 2000), 79–122.
4 Killick, *IMF Programs in Developing Countries*, 60.

5 Killick, *IMF Programs in Developing Countries*, 60.

6 Another important problem that is easily remedied goes as follows: Often countries face major exogenous shocks to their economy which make strict compliance with the original terms of an arrangement impossible. In some of these cases, countries are granted a waiver, where the loan is released even though original policy targets were not met. In other cases, the original arrangement is simply *cancelled* and replaced with a new arrangement with a new set of policy conditions. The government may comply with the new set of conditions, even though they failed to draw all of the resources in the original cancelled-arrangement. For more on this, see Martin S. Edwards, "Things Fall Apart: Why Do IMF Agreements Break Down?" Prepared for delivery at the Duke University Center for International Studies Conference International Institutions: Global Processes/Domestic Consequences, Durham, April 9–11, 1999.

7 Axel Dreher, "The Influence of Elections on IMF Programme Interruptions," *The Journal of Development Studies* 39 no. 6 (2003): 101–20.

8 Susan Schadler, *IMF Conditionality: Experiences Under Stand-By and Extended Arrangements, Part II: Background Papers, Occasional Paper 129* (Washington, DC: International Monetary Fund, 1995).

9 Economist Mauro Mecagni of the IMF considers similar "discontinuities" in loan disbursements of SAF and ESAF programs in 36 countries. Mauro Mecagni, "The Causes of Program Interruptions," in Hugh Bredenkamp and Susan Schadler, *Economic Adjustment and Reform in Low-Income Countries* (Washington, DC: International Monetary Fund, 1999), 215–76.

10 Martin Edwards, "Sticking with Yes: Domestic Institutions and IMF Compliance," mimeo, Rutgers University (2001); as cited in Axel Dreher, "IMF and Economic Growth: The Effects of Programs, Loans, and Compliance with Conditionality," *World Development*, 34 no. 5 (2006).

11 See Anna Ivanova, Wolfgang Mayer, Alex Mourmouras, and George Anayiotos, "What Determines the Success or Failure of Fund-Supported Programs?" IMF Working Paper, Policy Development and Review Department, authorized for distribution by Timothy D. Lane (November 2001); and Saleh M. Nsouli, Rouben Atoian, and Alex Mourmouras, "Institutions, Program Implementation, and Macroeconomic Performance," IMF Working Paper (04/184), IMF Institute and Middle East and Central Asia Department (September 2004).

12 Valerie Mercer-Blackman and Anna Unigovskaya, "Compliance with IMF Indicators and Growth in Transition Economies," IMF Working Paper (00/47), European II and Western Hemisphere Departments, authorized for distribution by Oleh Havrylyshyn and Juan Carlos Di Tata (March 2000).

13 Note that because in many cases the IMF may deem a country as partially compliant, Mercer-Blackman and Unigovskaya included in their indexes "partial credit" in cases where the IMF deemed that the condition was met "to a certain extent" or if it was "met after modification." They arbitrarily give exactly half credit to any condition that is partially achieved. For the Index of Fund Program Implementation they arbitrarily assign 30 percent credit for conditions that were waived after modification.

14 Nsouli, Atoian, and Mourmouras, "Institutions, Program Implementation, and Macroeconomic Performance," 26, table 2. Table 5.1 differs in some ways from the original table. The major change is that the "Overall

Implementation Index," which is constructed from the Quantitative and Structural Indexes, is left out. It is misleading to report the correlation between an index and the two components of the index – by construction such correlations will tend to be high. The other major change is that instead of reporting "Programs with irreversible interruptions," I report "Programs with no irreversible interruptions" so that the signs of the correlation coefficients are the same throughout the table.

15 W. A. Beveridge and M. R. Kelly, "Fiscal Content of Financial Programs Supported by Stand-By Arrangements in the Upper Credit Tranches, 1969–78," *IMF Staff Papers* 27 (1980), 205–49; as cited in Dreher, "IMF and Economic Growth."

16 Beveridge and Kelly, "Fiscal Content of Financial Programs Supported by Stand-By Arrangements in the Upper Credit Tranches, 1969–78," as reported in Jacques J. Polak, *The Changing Nature of IMF Conditionality*, Essay in International Finance No. 184 (Princeton, NJ: Princeton University, 1991).

17 Sebastian Edwards, "The International Monetary Fund and the Developing Countries: A Critical Evaluation," *Carnegie-Rochester Conference Series on Public Policy* 31 (1989): 7–68.

18 Edwards, "The International Monetary Fund and the Developing Countries: A Critical Evaluation," 30.

19 Justin B. Zulu and Saleh M. Nsouli, "Adjustment programs in Africa: the experience," *IMF Occasional Paper* 34 (1985); as cited in Dreher, "IMF and Economic Growth."

20 Erica Gould, "Money Talks: Supplementary Financiers and International Monetary Fund Conditionality," *International Organization* 57 no.3 (2003).

21 Polak, *The Changing Nature of IMF Conditionality*, 42–3.

22 Axel Dreher and Roland Vaubel, "The Causes and Consequences of IMF Conditionality," *Emerging Markets Finance and Trade* 40 no. 3 (2004): 26–54.

23 Ivanova, Mayer, Mourmouras, and Anayiotos, "What Determines the Success or Failure of Fund-Supported Programs?"

24 Nsouli, Atoian, and Mourmouras, "Institutions, Program Implementation, and Macroeconomic Performance."

25 Nsouli, Atoian, and Mourmouras, "Institutions, Program Implementation, and Macroeconomic Performance," 13.

26 Nsouli, Atoian, and Mourmouras, "Institutions, Program Implementation, and Macroeconomic Performance," 19.

27 It should be noted that most of these political variables come from International Country Risk Guide, which are not commonly used or accepted by political scientists.

28 Dreher, "IMF and Economic Growth," 769–88.

29 Joseph P. Joyce, "Promises Made, Promises Broken: A Model of IMF Program Implementation," *Economics and Politics* (forthcoming 2007). Also see Joseph P. Joyce, "Adoption, Implementation and Impact of IMF Programmes: A Review of the Issues and Evidence," *Comparative Economic Studies* 46 no. 3 (2004): 451–67.

30 Dreher, Sturm, and Vreeland, "Does Membership on the UN Security Council Influence IMF decisions?"

31 In a related study, (Axel Dreher, "Does the IMF Influence Fiscal and Monetary Policy?" *The Journal of Policy Reform* 8 no. 3 (2005)) Dreher finds that IMF programs improve fiscal and monetary policy, however, the

policy change appears uncorrelated to IMF loan disbursements. This indicates that enforcement by the IMF is weak and that policy change may be
more domestically rooted.

32 Nsouli, Atoian, and Mourmouras, "Institutions, Program Implementation,
and Macroeconomic Performance."

6 Reform the IMF?

1 Before this, there were many on the political left who had been quite vocal
in their opposition to the IMF. See, for example, the viewpoints of the 50
Years is Enough organization at www.50years.org.

2 Richard E. Feinberg, "The Changing Relationship between the World
Bank and the International Monetary Fund," *International Organization*
42 no. 3 (1988): 545–60.

3 Note that there are many who have criticized the IMF. Many of the
critiques repeat themselves, so, in the interest of space, most of them are
not listed here. I employ the left-right device as a way to simplify the
debate. There are, of course, many nuances that do not fit well within this
rubric, and even what one considers to be "left" or "right" depends on
one's point of view.

4 Joseph Stiglitz, *Globalization and Its Discontents* (New York: Norton,
2003). There are, of course, critics considered further to the political left
than Stiglitz – a political spectrum itself tends to depend on the cultural
context. Someone who appears to the left in the US may be considered
moderate in some European or Latin American countries. For someone
recognizably to the left of the political spectrum in Europe, for example,
see Richard Peet, *Unholy Trinity: The IMF, World Bank and WTO* (New
York: Zed Books, 2003).

5 For others that view the problem with IMF programs as the policies, see,
for example, Jeffrey Sachs, "How to Run the International Monetary
Fund," *Foreign Affairs* (July–August 2004): 60–4; William Easterly, "An
Identity Crisis? Testing IMF Financial Programming," *Center for Global
Development Working Paper* 9 (2002); and Ajit Singh, "'Asian Capitalism'
and the Financial Crisis," in Jonathan Michie and John Grieve Smith,
Global Instability: The Political Economy of World Economic Governance
(New York: Routledge, 1999), 9–36.

6 Stiglitz, *Globalization and Its Discontents*, 201.

7 See, for example, Stiglitz, *Globalization and Its Discontents*, 84.

8 Stiglitz, *Globalization and Its Discontents*, 240.

9 Stiglitz, *Globalization and Its Discontents*, 206.

10 Stiglitz, *Globalization and Its Discontents*, 240.

11 Stiglitz, *Globalization and Its Discontents*, 226. For a compelling argument
in favor of better representation at the Fund, see Devesh Kapur, "Who Gets
to Run the World," *Foreign Policy* (November/December 2000): 44–50.

12 Ngaire Woods, "Making the IMF and the World Bank More Accountable,"
in Ariel Buira, *Reforming the Governance of the IMF and the World Bank*
(London: Anthem Press 2005), 149–70.

13 "Reality Check at the IMF," *The Economist* (April 22–28, 2006): 12, 14.

14 Ariel Buira, "The Bretton Woods Institutions: Governance without
Legitimacy?" in Ariel Buira, *Reforming the Governance of the IMF and the*

World Bank (London: Anthem Press, 2005), 7–44. See also Graham Bird and Dane Rowlands, "IMF Quotas: Constructing an International Organization using Inferior Building Blocks," *The Review of International Organizations* 1 no. 2 (2006): 153 – 71.

15 See the article cited in Note 13, "Reality Check at the IMF," 12,14.

16 James Tobin, "Financial Globalization: Can National Currencies Survive?" in *Annual World Bank Conference on Development Economics 1998*, ed., Boris Pleskovic and Joseph E. Stiglitz (Washington, DC: The World Bank, 1998).

17 See Bessma Momani, "Recruiting and Diversifying IMF Technocrats," *Global Society* 19 no. 2 (April 2005): 167–87.

18 Joseph Stiglitz, "Reflections on the Theory and Practice of Reform," in Anne O. Krueger, *Economic Policy Reform: The Second Stage* (Chicago, IL: The University of Chicago Press, 2000), 551.

19 See Robert Dahl, "Can International Organizations be Democratic? A skeptic's view," in Ian Shapiro and Casiano Hacker-Cordon, *Democracy's Edges* (New York: Cambridge University Press, 1999), 19–36. But also consider the suggestion of Bruno S. Frey and Alois Stutzer of the University of Zurich, who propose that a representative sample of citizen "trustees," selected using a random mechanism, play a role in the actual governance of international institutions. Bruno S. Frey and Alois Stutzer, "Strengthening the citizens' role in international organizations," *The Review of International Organizations* 1 no. 1 (March 2006): 27–43.

20 See also Roland Vaubel, "Principal Agent Problems in International Organizations," *The Review of International Organizations* 1 no. 2 (2006): 125–38.

21 For related ideas about the connections between democracy and the IMF, see Devesh Kapur and Moises Naim, "The IMF and Democratic Governance," *Journal of Democracy* 16 no. 1 (January 2005).

22 This description of the evolution of thinking about domestic politics follows Barry Eichengreen, *Toward a New International Financial Architecture* (Washington, DC: Institute for International Economics, 1999), 133–41.

23 Eichengreen, *Toward a New International Financial Architecture*.

24 Eichengreen, *Toward a New International Financial Architecture*.

25 See Meltzer Commission, "Report of the International Financial Institution Advisory Commission to the US Congress," (2000). For a recent discussion of Meltzer's views, see the exchange between him and former IMF First Deputy Managing Director Anne Krueger: Allan H. Meltzer, "Reviving the Bank and Fund," *The Review of International Organizations* 1 no. 1 (March 2006): 49–59. Anne O. Krueger, "A Response to Allan Meltzer," *The Review of International Organizations* 1 no. 1 (March 2006): 61–4. Allan H. Meltzer, "Reply to Anne Krueger," *The Review of International Organizations* 1 no. 1 (March 2006): 65–7.

26 Thomas Willett, "Understanding the IMF Debate," *Independent Review* 5 no. 4 (2001): 593–610.

27 See, for example, Kenneth Rogoff, "The Sisters at 60," *The Economist* (24 July 2004): 65–7; and Stanley Fischer, *IMF Essays from a Time of Crisis: The International Financial System, Stabilization and Development* (Cambridge, MA: MIT Press, 2004).

28 Mohsin Khan and Sunil Sharma "IMF Conditionality and Country Ownership of Programs," IMF Working Paper 01/142 (September 2001), 13–14. For a more radical type of ownership, called "self-imposed conditionality," see the work of New York University law professor Ofer Eldar, "Reform of IMF Conditionality: A Proposal for Self-Imposed Conditionality," *Journal of International Economic Law* 8 no. 2 (2005): 509–49.

29 IMF, "The Fund's Transparency Policy – Review of the Experience and Next Steps," Prepared by the Policy Development and Review Department (in consultation with the External Relations and other Departments), 24 May 2002.

30 IMF, "Conditionality in Fund-Supported Programs."

31 Note, however, that this is not entirely new either. Citing Jan Aart Scholte, "The IMF Meets Civil Society," *Finance and Development* 35, no. 3 (1998), Rorden Wilkinson and Steve Hughes report that the IMF has been reaching out to, or at least informing, labor, business, agricultural, and religious organizations as well as NGOs as far back as 1996. Rorden Wilkinson and Steve Hughes, "Labor Standards and Global Governance: Examining the Dimensions Of Institutional Engagement," *Global Governance* no. 2 (2000): 259–77.

32 See, for example, Executive Board Public Information Notice (PIN) No. 02/30 of March 15, 2002; The IEO Report on the Evaluation of Poverty Reduction Strategy Papers (PRSPs) and The Poverty Reduction and Growth Facility (PRGF); and the September 2005 IMF Factsheet on The Poverty Reduction and Growth Facility (PRGF) available at www.imf.org.

33 A study of the effects of programs under the PRGF's predecessor, the ESAF from 1986 to 1991 by Louis Dicks-Mireaux, Mauro Mecagni, and Susan Schadler of the IMF Policy Development and Review Department showed that if the IMF has had a positive impact on growth anywhere, it may be under these programs. The IMF stresses, however, that per capita income in participant countries remains low, so participation should be expected to continue. See Dicks-Mireaux, Mecagni, and Schadler, "Evaluating the Effect of IMF Lending to Low Income Countries."

Conclusion

1 De Rato's team reflects his views on global governance – it includes one central banker from the United States, one from South Africa, one from Mexico, one from Saudi Arabia, one from Europe, one from China, and is chaired by a private finance representative.

2 This idea comes directly from Dreher, Sturm, and Vreeland, "Does membership on the UN Security Council influence IMF decisions?"

3 See Jon Elster, *Ulysses Unbound: Studies in Rationality, Precommitment, and Constraints* (New York: Cambridge University Press, 2000).

4 IMF, "The Managing Director's Report on Implementing the Fund's Medium-Term Strategy" (April 5, 2006), 1.

5 IMF, "The Managing Director's Report," 2.

6 IMF, "The Managing Director's Report," 2.

Select bibliography

Graham Bird, *IMF Lending to Developing Countries, Issues and Evidence* (London: Routledge, 1995). Published in 1995, it remains an excellent introduction to the historical patterns of IMF lending. Accessible yet sophisticated and detailed.

James M. Boughton, *Silent Revolution: The International Monetary Fund, 1979–1989* (Washington, DC: IMF, 2001). A thorough history of a transition period of the IMF, this book is informative and a pleasure to read – authored by the IMF economic historian.

Barry Eichengreen, *Globalizing Capital: A History of the International Monetary System* (Princeton, NJ: Princeton University Press, 1998). This book is worth studying carefully and reading more than once. Each read will teach something new about how international monetary relationships evolved over the course of the twentieth century. An understanding of the ideas in this book is required to understand what and why the IMF is.

Norman K. Humphreys, *Historical Dictionary of the International Monetary Fund, Second Edition* (Lanham, MD: Scarecrow Press, 1999). This is a handy reference tool to look up various technical terms employed – particularly useful to those new to the study of the IMF.

Manuel Pastor, *The International Monetary Fund and Latin America: Economic Stabilization and Class Conflict* (Boulder, CO: Westview Press, 1987). The first thorough, systematic study on the distributional consequences of IMF programs. It focuses on Latin America's long history with IMF programs up through the Debt Crisis.

Gustav Ranis, James Raymond Vreeland, and Stephen Kosack, *Globalization and the Nation State: The Impact of the IMF and the World Bank* (New York: Routledge, 2006). This volume presents the cutting edge of research on political factors that influence the International Monetary Fund and the World Bank, reevaluating the conventional wisdom on why countries enter into structural adjustment programs and with what effects.

Joseph Stiglitz, *Globalization and Its Discontents* (New York: Norton, 2003). By far the most cited and most widely read book referenced here. Stiglitz is a Nobel Prize winning economist who was on the inside of World Bank and IMF negotiations during the East Asian Financial Crisis. He apparently holds nothing back in this book.

Strom Thacker, "The High Politics of IMF Lending," *World Politics* 52 no. 1 (1999): 38–75. A path-breaking study of US political influence over the IMF in that it is the first to use systematic data.

Roland Vaubel, "A Public Choice Approach to International Organization," *Public Choice* 51 no. 1 (1986): 39–57. This article is one of the early publications in a body of Vaubel's work on the bureaucratic incentives of the IMF. The work highlights the problem of the non-accountability of the IMF.

John Williamson, *IMF Conditionality* (Washington, DC: Institute for International Economics, 1983). This edited volume is filled with 21 contributions on the IMF. Authors include some of the most important researchers on the IMF, and many of the chapters are among the most referenced in the IMF literature.

Morris Goldstein and Peter J. Montiel, "Evaluating Fund Stabilization Programs with Multicountry Data: Some Methodological Pitfalls," *IMF Staff Papers* 33 (June 1986): 304–44. This article provides a technical overview of various methodological approaches to evaluating IMF programs – essential reading for the statistical analysis of IMF impacts.

Essential Internet based resources

Joseph P. Joyce, International Financial Institutions Research Site, www.wellesley. edu/Economics/IFI/index.html. This webpage lists the most important reference books, books and monographs, and published articles on the IMF. For those interested in further research on the IMF, this is the place to start.

IMF, International Monetary Fund Webpage, www.imf.org. Much of the IMF's own research is published on this webpage, as well as Letters of Intent, *IMF Annual Reports*, press releases, introductory and advanced information about the IMF for students and journalists, IMF finance information, and member country economic information.

Index

Note: 'b' refers to box, 'n' to note and 't' to table.

GLOBAL INSTITUTIONS SERIES

NEW TITLE
The North Atlantic Treaty Organization
The Enduring Alliance

Julian Lindley-French, Center for Applied Policy, Munich, Germany

The North Atlantic Treaty Organization clearly outlines all of the institution's key facets to deliver an authoritative account. Detailing the origins, institutions, workings and activities of NATO, this volume also focuses on its future as the institutional basis for the security dimension of the transatlantic relationship, and an institution contributing to global security. It is clear that NATO faces fresh challenges in the twenty-first century and will be in the spotlight for years to come.

Contents
1. Introduction 2. The Origins of NATO 3. The Structure of NATO 4. NATO during the Cold War 5. NATO After the Cold War 6. NATO Goes Global? 7. Conclusion

November 2006: 216x138: 176pp
Hb: 978-0-415-35879-8: **£65.00**
Pb: 978-0-415-35880-4: **£14.99**

NEW TITLE
The Group of 7/8
Hugo Dobson, University of Sheffield, UK

Hugo Dobson's new book, *The Group of 7/8* is a highly accessible, up-to-date introduction to the history, present and future of the G7/8 summits. This book aims to explore the role that the G8 plays and will play on global governance. The general consensus amongst researchers is to deny that the G8 is an institution and should therefore not be included in topics such as global governance. Dobson describes it as the world's biggest think-tank on global governance, unlike any legalized established institutions, the Group of 7/8 acts as a forum where ideas can be floated, discuss, and if successful, delegated to the relevant body for implementations.

Contents
1. History and Development 2. Organization and Functioning 3. Perspectives of Member States 4. Achievements and Challenges 5. Criticisms and Challenges 6. Future Directions

December 2006: 216x138: 160pp
Hb: 978-0-415-37018-9: **£65.00**
Pb: 978-0-415-37014-1: **£14.99**

Routledge
Taylor & Francis Group

To order any of these titles
Call: +44 (0) 1264 34 3071
Fax: +44 (0) 1264 34 3005
Email: book.orders@routledge.co.uk

For further information visit:
www.routledge.com/politics

GLOBAL INSTITUTIONS SERIES

NEW TITLE
The World Economic Forum
A Multi-Stakeholder Approach to Global Governance

Dr Geoffrey Allen Pigman, Bennington College, Vermont, USA

This book explores the paradoxes and unique characteristics of the World Economic Forum, highlighting contemporary issues and debates on global governance, economic development, and corporate social responsibility.

Contents
1. A Multi-Stakeholder Approach: An Historical Overview 2. Purposes Public and Private: How the Forum Works 3. The Forum in Contemporary Global Society: Theoretical Questions 4. Generating Knowledge Today: WEF Meetings in 2005 5. Discourse, Research and Action: Technology and the Initiatives 6. Engaging the Critics 7. The Forum Looking Ahead

December 2006: 216x138: 208pp
Hb: 978-0-415-70203-4: **£65.00**
Pb: 978-0-415-70204-1: **£14.99**

FORTHCOMING TITLE
The International Committee of Red Cross
A Neutral Humanitarian Actor

David P. Forsythe, University of Nebraska-Lincoln, USA and
Barbara Ann J. Rieffer-Flanagan, Central Washington University, USA

The International Committee of the Red Cross analyses international humanitarian action as practiced by the International Red Cross. This entails explaining its history and structure as well as examining contemporary field experience and broad diplomatic initiatives related to its principal tasks.

Contents
1. The Historical Development of the ICRC 2. ICRC Organization and Management 3. The ICRC and International Humanitarian Law 4. Humanitarian Assistance and Restoration of Family Ties 5. Detention Visits 6. The Future of the ICRC

March 2007: 216x138: 144pp
Hb: 978-0-415-34613-9: **£65.00**
Pb: 978-0-415-34151-6: **£14.99**

Routledge
Taylor & Francis Group

To order any of these titles
Call: +44 (0) 1264 34 3071
Fax: +44 (0) 1264 34 3005
Email: book.orders@routledge.co.uk

For further information visit:
www.routledge.com/politics

GLOBAL INSTITUTIONS SERIES

FORTHCOMING TITLE

A Crisis in Global Institutions?

Multilateralism and International Security

Edward Newman, United Nations University, Tokyo

This volume considers if there is a crisis in global institutions which address security challenges, exploring the sources of these challenges and how multilateralism might be more viably constituted to cope with contemporary and future demands.

Contents

1. Introduction 2. Defining the Crisis of Multilateralism in the Area of International Peace and Security 3. Sources of the Crisis of Multilateralism 4. Emerging Alternatives to the Existing Values and Institutions of Multilateralism 5. New Multilateralism? Towards a 'Post-Westphalian' Model of Multilateralism 6. Conclusion

June 2007: 234x156: 184pp
Hb: 978-0-415-41164-6: **£65.00**
Pb: 978-0-415-41165-3: **£16.99**

FORTHCOMING TITLE

Organisation for Security and Co-operation in Europe (OSCE)

David Galbreath, University of Aberdeen, UK

This volume examines the development and evolution of the Organization of Security and Cooperation in Europe during and after the Cold War. This title sheds light on an institution that changed the face of global security during the Cold War and championed the rise of democratization in Central and Eastern Europe as well as the former Soviet republics following the collapse of the Soviet Union.

Contents

1. European Security and Cooperation in Context 2. The Helsinki Final Act and Comprehensive Security 3. From "Conference" to "Organization" 4. Security Management 5. Democratization and Human Rights 6. The OSCE and the European Security Architecture 7. Crisis? What Crisis?

September 2007: 216x138: 224pp
Hb: 978-0-415-40763-2: **£65.00**
Pb: 978-0-415-40764-9: **£16.99**

Routledge
Taylor & Francis Group

To order any of these titles
Call: +44 (0) 1264 34 3071
Fax: +44 (0) 1264 34 3005
Email: book.orders@routledge.co.uk

For further information visit:
www.routledge.com/politics